BECOMING
AN AWESOME
PRODUCT OWNER

DEVELOPING PRODUCTS IN
THE **AGILE** WAY

ANUSHA HEWAGE

DEDICATION

To My Mother

TABLE OF CONTENTS

INTRODUCTION
AGILE & PRODUCT DEVELOPMENT

The term 'Product Owner' (PO) was not popular until the last decade. In 2007, when I was developing a very large software product for an airline company, nobody introduced me as a Product Owner. But a decade later, we can find many Product Owners, and that is thanks to the widespread use of 'Agile' in the services industry. Most organizations have embraced Agile as a new way of working. This indicates a shift towards a different working mindset, which is a promising trend.

In Agile, delivering value to the customer becomes the focus. Agile does that by unleashing the potential of all people associated with the process, especially the employees. Hence Agile builds a happy working environment for people. And this is an important factor all leaders should think about.

Research demonstrates that today's younger workforce, the millennials, and the future workforce have different considerations than the previous generations when they choose which employers to work with. 'Purpose', 'impact' and 'autonomy' matter to them. Their workplaces are vibrant, less hierarchical and becoming more and more so. In such organizations, hierarchies disappear. Leadership styles change, so much so that CEOs are seated at hot desks instead of corner offices. T-shirts and jeans become the preferred office-wear rather than suits. Agile transforms workplaces to happy places.

Thanks to Agile, and this new way of working, the focus of business has shifted to finding ways to deliver faster and better value to the customer. After reading the Agile manifesto, and Agile principles and practices, organizational leaders have started becoming familiar with the word 'Scrum' and wondering how they can implement this in their workplaces.

Transitioning to Agile

Transition to Agile is on the agenda of almost all organizations, whether they are big or small. Some recent converts are 3M, IBM, DBS Bank (Singapore), British Petroleum, and Accenture. I know about these organizations because I have worked with them either as an employee or as an Agile Transformation Leader. Some other companies that have transitioned to Agile are ING Bank, Netflix, Google, Microsoft and Amazon.

Why the hype?

But why all this hype about Agile? Why does every organization want to absorb Agile as a new way of working? We can turn towards some research data to find an answer. Standish Group conducted research on project success based on organizations' project delivery methodology: Waterfall and Agile. This research provides us with very interesting findings. According to the research, Agile-based projects have had greater success compared to those that used Waterfall as depicted in Table 1 below.

METHOD	SUCCESSFUL	CHALLENGED	FAILED
Agile	39%	52%	9%
Waterfall	11%	60%	29%

Table 1: Comparison of Agile- and Waterfall- based project successes (Standish Group, 2015)

As evident from the table above, projects that used Agile had three times the success rate compared to those that used Waterfall, which had a higher failure rate.

There are further insights from the Standish Group research. Depending on the size of the projects, there seems to be a co-relation between the project success and its methodology as depicted in the table below.

Project Size	Type	Successful	Challenged	Failed
Large	Agile	18%	59%	23%
	Waterfall	3%	55%	42%
Medium	Agile	27%	62%	11%
	Waterfall	7%	68%	25%
Small	Agile	58%	38%	4%
	Waterfall	44%	45%	11%

Table 2: Comparison of small, medium, and large projects using Agile and Waterfall (Standish Group, 2015)

As is obvious from the table above, nearly half the large-scale projects that used Waterfall as a methodology have failed. But with Agile, only one project out of four failed. If we assume these projects cost five million each, nearly ten million (two projects) have been spent without success (a sunk cost). Looking at small scale projects (let's say there are less than ten people in the team) which cost only a 100,000 each, only four such projects out of hundred would fail. That is only 400,000 sunk costs. But if the PO used Waterfall instead of Agile for these projects, eleven projects would fail and that is 1.1 million sunk costs.

Hence, comparatively speaking, there is enough evidence to prove the success of Agile as a methodology over any other type. However, Agile, too, does not have a hundred per cent success. Even Agile-based projects have failed, although the percentage is much smaller. If I were a business owner, I would not want any projects to fail as they are huge investments. So, let's see why Agile fails sometimes.

When does Agile fail?

Statistics and research findings help us to conclude that Agile is no magic wand which when waved will make a project successful. Even some Agile-based projects have failed. Why?

To answer this question, I did some research where I spoke to industry experts who implemented Agile in their small to large organizations. I also studied existing literature. These research findings resonated with my industry experience and insights generated while working on Agile transformation initiatives.

One interesting finding is linked to the transitioning steps taken to move to Agile. Miloš Jovanovic et al. (2017) say 'most organizations focus on the desired outcome of the Agile implementation rather than the necessary steps to get there'. This means that leaders expect overnight results from Agile, often forgetting that a step-by-step process is required to be really agile!

Nerur et al. (2005) in the research, identified four groups of challenges during the Agile method adoption: management and organizational, people, process, and technology. They further narrow down the issues found in organizational culture, management style, organizational form, management and/or development knowledge and reward system. Naturally, when an organization transitions to Agile, a change in the management style is also necessary. Are the managers ready to be the agents of the change that comes with Agile? Are they equipped to change, for example, from linear hierarchies to flat or lean hierarchies? Moreover, the measure of performance in an Agile environment is completely different from what is used for other methodologies. It cannot be the same carrot-and-stick approach which traditional organizations use. Are organizations taking these necessary steps to ensure a smooth transition to Agile?

Further research was conducted by scholars such as Campanelli and Silva Parreiras on the subject of challenges around adopting Agile practices. They conclude 'the complexity of adopting Agile practices is high, because of resistance to change, the necessity of higher management involvement and organizational culture' (Campanelli and Silva Parreiras, 2015; Cao et al., 2009; Dyba and Dingsoyr, 2009).

The confusion around functional roles is also a contributing factor to the failure of Agile-based projects. Stettina and Hörz conclude: 'Interplay of practices across functional roles should be better understood in order to comprehend organizational agility' (Stettina and Hörz,

2014). 'Larger software development organizations tend to have more organizational roles, while smaller companies tend to merge roles in a manner to create the best fit to their operations limitation' (Yilmaz et al., 2015).

One of the main confusions during Agile adaptation is about role mapping. Agile comes with many new role definitions: **Scrum Master, Product Owner, Area Product Owner (APO), Agile Release Train Engineer**, to name a few. However, traditional organizations define managerial positions as: Program Manager, Project Manager, Product Manager, Business Analysts, Software Engineer, Software Tester, Division Manager, etc. What happens to these roles when Agile is implemented? In most cases, traditional roles are directly mapped to the new Agile project team without any proper study or training that might prepare them to take on the new role.

Research was conducted by Milos Jovanovic et al. (2017) on organizations that implemented Agile. They interviewed five different Agile teams on their Agile role mapping experience, and this revealed the following.

Team	Old Role	New Agile Role
T1	Systems Architect	Product Owner
T1	Software Developer	Scrum Master
T2	Systems Architect	Product Owner
T2	Systems Architect	Scrum Master
T3	Project Manager	Product Owner
T3	Software Developer	Scrum Master
T4	Project Manager	Product Owner
T4	Requirements Engineer	Scrum Master
T5	Project Manager	Product Owner
T5	Requirements Engineer	Scrum Master

Table 3: Participant team members and role mapping (Milos Jovanovic et al., 2017)

The above research was conducted with more than 350 employees in Spain who work with more than 3,000 tourism sector clients. Let's consider this a small company in comparison with a multinational company, for example, which has more than 200,000 employees. As an Agile practitioner with more than ten years of hands-on experience with big companies as clients, I am not surprised by the above data, as my personal experience has been the same. Project Managers are mapped into Scrum Masters; Business Analysts are mapped into Product Owner and so on. These role mappings are insane. No wonder some Agile projects are challenged and some failed.

The critical role of the Product Owner

I have worked in many small and large companies around the world. Most of them have transitioned to Agile in the last decade. My observation has been that a Product Owner's role is often misunderstood in a company's shift to Agile. This is one of the most critical roles for the success of any product a team may be working on. Unfortunately, organizations do not pay enough attention to this. As a result, many products fail to produce any return on investment although the product development methodology is Agile.

Product Owner is the leadership position of an Agile team and is the voice of the customer. Hence the Product Owner must have very good knowledge of Agile processes, practices and the product development process. As a practitioner I find that there is a gap in the industry. Product Owners with this knowledge are rare. The intention of this book is to provide Product Owners with very good knowledge from a practical standpoint.

References

Chaos Report, 2015, The Standish Group International

Miloš Jovanović, Antonia Mas, Antoni-Lluís Mesquida, Bojan Lalić,Transition of organizational roles in Agile transformation process: A grounded theory approach, Journal of Systems and Software, Volume 133,2017,Pages 174-194,ISSN 0164-1212,

CHAPTER 1
AGILE PRODUCT DEVELOPMENT

What is Agile?

I t is important to understand Agile before we talk about the Product Owner and the Agile way of Product Development. To answer this question, I need to introduce you to the traditional way of developing products.

Traditional product development

Before Agile became a leading way of developing software products, there was 'Waterfall', which is a phased-gate approach to doing the same. Let me tell you a story where I experienced this approach as a software engineer a long time ago. Let's call the consultancy company I worked at 'Super IT'. People like myself were hired to develop software for a bank; let's call it 'Best Bank'. Here is what happened during the process of developing software for 'Best Bank'.

At 'Super IT', the team was composed of a few software engineers (I was one of them), a business analyst, quality assurance engineers (testers), a technical lead and a project manager. We occupied a small office in the Super IT building. One fine day, our project manager came to us and announced that we had won a contract with Best Bank. Being new in the field, the team had no clue as to who or what Best Bank was. Naturally, we did not understand what the big deal was.

The project commenced the next day, and our business analyst and project manager went to meet the Best Bank team and returned after a couple of days. We did not know any details yet. Suddenly, the project manager, business analyst and the technical lead became very busy. We hardly talked to them. Out of the three musketeers, the business analyst seemed particularly occupied and I had the impression that he was writing a book. All three sat in the office even after office hours, and also during the weekends. Finally, they sent us a copy of the documents they created: User Requirement Specification (URS) and Product Solution Proposal. They asked us to read and understand it. The sheer volume of the documents was staggering. Having given us the documents, they were gone again for another week and we forgot about this Best Bank encyclopedia.

When the musketeers returned after one week, the looks on their faces were those of children who have been scolded by their teachers. Something must have happened, we gossiped. They got busy again, and after a few weeks, they went back to Best Bank. This kept happening repeatedly until finally they called us to the conference room and said: 'We've won the contract. We'll send you the new URS and solution proposal. The product has to be built in two months. So we'll begin work tomorrow. Be ready guys, the faster we build it, the better.' We looked at each other, but didn't say anything because they didn't ask our opinion.

The next two months were an interesting period of my career. Our business analyst gave us a copy of the new URS as the customer had thrown away what he had prepared as the first draft, saying it was not what they wanted. Within a day, he explained to us the software requirements he had gathered over two months. The following day, our technical lead explained to us the architecture of the solution we were to build. We were scared to say we did not understand anything, because when we asked questions, the business analyst would say: 'Be smart; this is not rocket science'.

We finally started work—spending days and nights, weekdays and weekends building that software. The project manager kept on assigning us impossible tasks. When I wanted one whole day to develop the web page, he gave me just two hours. Every thirty minutes he would come and ask: 'Is it finished?' We did not have time to think about quality; we simply tried to squeeze one day of code writing into two hours and save ourselves from public embarrassment. We were tired and exhausted throughout. After two months, when the task was finished, we were all relieved.

The following week, the entire team went to Best Bank to show the software to them. That was the first time the whole team was meeting them. Best Bank insisted on doing user acceptance testing (UAT). We were skeptical about the whole thing. Our project manager, business analyst and the technical lead, took the lead to explain to Best Bank the solution we had built for them. When they made mistakes in the presentation, we looked at each other. They missed out a lot of things; if we were to explain the solution, we could have done it much better. But we were not allowed to talk. Finally, we installed the software on the clients' machines and asked them to test it.

In the first instance, it was a disaster. The software did not load on Best Bank's machines. I clearly remember that incident because everyone was looking at us for explanation when it failed to load. Finally, our technical lead did something and it loaded to everyone's relief. The next thing I remember is the client's high-pitched question: 'What is this?' This person must have been the business manager, and he was addressing our project manager and waiting for an answer. When our project manager did not respond, he kept nodding his head and saying: 'This is not what we wanted. You've got it wrong'. At this point, our business analyst opened the URS and turned the pages to explain that we had built exactly what Best Bank had explained to us. But they were not happy; they kept saying: 'That was not what we meant'.

When the day was over, we were all exhausted and disappointed. There were no words to explain how we felt. We had spent days and nights, weekdays and weekends just to hear 'this is not what we wanted'? The next day we started rebuilding the same thing, **again**! This was how software products was developed most of the time.

Traditional software development is a nightmare

Software development using the traditional method is a nightmare. It is a nightmare for the team members working on building it, and the customers. This storyline has not changed much after two decades. The reason for this is the way traditional software development is structured. It is a phase-by-phase approach, as illustrated in the figure below.

Figure 1: Traditional software development cycle

Because of the way it has been structured, the traditional software development cycle is longer. As a result, when the customer eventually gets the product, a few months, sometimes even a few years, have passed. Also, the customer is less engaged in the phases of product development. It is a siloed approach where a software development team works in isolation and the customer is engaged with only at the end, during user acceptance testing. A bunch of documents are created throughout the process, and more efforts are directed towards creating these documents instead of developing the product. Hence, we find that this traditional way of developing software is a waste of time, money, and effort and causes trouble for the customer as well as the development team.

This is the main reason why Agile is so effective. It introduces a new way of working as well as of developing products. Agile and product development go hand-in-hand. But before we consider the link between the two, let us examine product development and Agile as two separate units.

Why do we develop products?

Products provide a unique service to consumers. Take, for example, a mobile phone. It allows us to be connected to anyone who also holds a phone, regardless of the geographical location, as long as network coverage is available. Now let us take network as a product. The mobile phone itself is useless unless there is a telecommunications network. So, it is as much the telecommunications network that allows people to be connected via devices like mobile phones. Each of these products provides a unique service to its user.

However, there are many products that provide the same service. For example, there are many models of mobile phones developed by various companies. Customers choose from the variety available, and more often than not, they choose products that provide maximum value for their money. Hence, if the product delivers high value, then the customer will purchase it.

However, providing value to the customer is extremely difficult, because what each customer values is different. One person's requirements may be different from another. For example, I may prefer a phone which has a longer battery life than a slim, fancy phone because I travel a lot. While I am on the move, I do not want to carry power banks and chargers etc., which make my luggage heavy. Hence, I prefer a phone which lasts for at least five days on a single charge. So, that is the value I expect the product to deliver to me. Another person's choice could be entirely different, based on their needs and requirements.

Products or services are the breadwinners of a business. Companies sell products and services to customers who need them, and the customers pay money in exchange. Hence, producing products which deliver value and producing those faster keeps the business competitive, and profitable. That means if a company can produce valued-based products in a short period of time, they are going to beat a competitor who does not do the same.

Concept of critical path

Speed matters; faster is better. But is it possible to fast-track product development? The answer is obvious from the current global pandemic of COVID-19, which began in 2020.

In this situation, the world desperately needs just one product: a miracle vaccine. But no one is able to develop it at the speed at which the world needs it. Not with the entire world's money or with any political party's power. But the world still desperately needs it. Had it been available while thousands of people around the world were dying, it could have saved lives. It could have saved people's jobs. It could have saved some companies from bankruptcy and saved the world from economic meltdown. But we have to wait. A vaccine could not be developed at the speed which the world expected. This is a very good example of the fact that no matter how much money there is to spend, how much power or effort, certain things cannot be done at the speed we want. But why couldn't the vaccine be developed at the speed we wanted? The answer lies with the process that has to be followed.

The vaccine needs to be developed first, and then it needs to be tested in laboratories under strict vigilance. If the hypothesis is proven, then it needs to be tested on animals. If it is proven appropriate, then a voluntary human trial can begin. Only if the trial data proves successful can the vaccine be made available for consumption under medical supervision, after receiving the necessary approvals from the health authorities. This long drawn out process is necessary to ensure that the vaccine stamps out the COVID-19 virus, and does not harm humans in any way, including any side effects.

Time to market

With the above example, it is clear that the time required to develop a product and the time to market it are both very critical factors in business. Customers need products faster than they can be produced. But product development is a time-consuming process. Also, finding the balance between production time and marketing time is really important to provide value to the customer. What every business tries to do is to shorten the development time as well as marketing time in an effort to deliver the product faster to the customer.

However, while doing this, it is important not to cut corners or compromise on the quality of the product. If customers do not find the product 'valuable' they will not buy it, which means the business may not even cover production costs.

Hence, while product development needs to be quick, at the same time, it should also deliver the quality the customer is expecting. That is where the Agile product development process comes into the picture.

Agile product development

As mentioned in the introduction chapter, there is enough research to prove the success of the Agile product development process. Since the focus of this book is to guide Product Owners through this development process, the next section of this book introduces Agile to Product Owners. What is explained here are the basic essentials for a Product Owner.

Some of the concepts I have explained below are extracted from various Agile frameworks. Some others are purely my personal view of how product development should take place. During my work, the times when I used a non-Agile way for product development were difficult experiences, even though they produced expected results. However, when I have used Agile, the success has been phenomenal. Some of the products were delivered even before the promised target date. And these products exceeded customer expectations. The product development journey was profitable and pleasurable, and the best part is that the returns on investment for those products were high compared to the marginal returns on investment from non-Agile methods of product development. This aligns with the academic research done by institutes and professional bodies. Hence, I highly recommend that Product Owners pay close attention to the Agile way of developing products.

More about Agile

When someone asks this question, 'what is Agile?', my answer is always very simple and consistent. **Agile is a mindset.** It is all about focusing on **delivering value to customers as early as possible.** It is about how we respond positively to the customers' needs. It is also about being flexible. It is about minimizing waste in the process of creating products. It is leveraging the team to use their expertise in the product development process. It is all about partnering with the customers, suppliers, and various teams to develop products that customers will love.

But 'being agile' is one of the hardest things to do! Simply because it is a change in the state of mind; it is about **changing behaviors.** Something like getting into the habit of going to the gym every day, or trying suddenly to stop smoking after being a chain-smoker for years—these are habitual changes, and not easy to make. We know they can be made, and the impact of doing them is phenomenal; but they are extremely hard. Adapting to Agile is something similar. Switching over from the old habits of product development to cultivating new mindsets and living them is extremely hard but doable, and, once done, benefits will emerge from every direction.

There are a few concepts which, when absorbed, help to change the mindset of how we look at some of the work/activities that we do in the process of being agile. That is where the Agile manifesto comes into the picture.

Agile manifesto

The reply I always get from any leader when I talk about the Agile manifesto is: 'I already know it.' However, only very few people understand the real meaning behind it.

The agile manifesto is the philosophy behind everything. It is the summarization of how to increase the value or quality for the customer by minimizing the waste in the process. Thus, I urge you to understand the underlying philosophy behind this manifesto before doing anything else.

The birth of the Agile manifesto goes back to 2001. Seventeen people who called themselves 'independent thinkers' got together and discussed how to make software even better. Since they were already practitioners of IT and software development, they knew what they were doing. They wanted to develop a new software that would be better than the old and traditional way which was not sustainable, productive, profitable, or enjoyable.

After two days of arguments, discussions, and exchange of opinions, they came up with the Agile manifesto. The strongest feature about Agile is that it was not something created by people who do not understand the software development process. Rather, it was created by those who were deeply involved in developing software products and who understood the difficulties faced in the traditional way of developing them. These experts strongly believed in finding a better way to do this.

The underlying philosophy of the Agile manifesto is the ease of the software development process. Although it was originally developed for software, the same principles apply to almost all types of products. Let's try to understand this philosophy which is the building block of the process that Product Owners follow to develop the product.

Individuals and interactions over processes and tools
Working software over comprehensive documentation
Customer collaboration over contract negotiation
Responding to change over following a plan

Agile manifesto (Agilemanifesto.org)

Individuals and interactions over processes and tools

Processes have a significant place in the corporate world. We have often heard phrases like, 'It is the process', 'We have to follow due process', 'That is how things are done here', 'Cannot bypass the process', and 'Processes are there for a reason' etc. While some of these processes are essential, in my experience most of these processes are followed simply for the sake of following the process.

In the corporate world, some of these processes have been given unnecessary priority. Processes should help to make things better, but when these processes are blindly followed, they make things unproductive. Unnecessary processes add delays to the end-to-end process. As a result, value delivery to the customer is delayed. The funny part is that most of the time, people do not know why such processes exist in the first place.

As an example, in one of the organizations I know, they had one of the longest employee recruitments cycles I have come across. When we wanted to recruit an employee in Australia, the approval had to be given by someone sitting in the Netherlands and nobody knew why it had to be like that. The person in the Netherlands received requests from all over the world. This resulted in delays due to the number of requests as well as the time zone difference.

In such situations, processes become a burden rather than an aid. That is why it is important to prioritize in order to get things done faster and better, with more individual and face-to-face interactions.

Why individuals and interactions?

Processes and tools do not talk to people. People are left behind every time we give precedence to processes and tools. Processes direct people to send emails or direct them to portals or to talk to chatbots; processes and tools are machineries. They do not have emotions. They cannot analyze a situation that has not occurred before and take actions based on the new situation. Processes have been created to suit average scenarios or common scenarios but most of the time, they fail to cater for exceptions.

But humans are the opposite of that. Humans are emotional; they are extremely complicated. And they react differently to different situations. These complicated people are the main asset we have in our workplaces. So, we have to find ways to engage with them and work with these complicated, emotional people rather than processes. Therefore, the best way to get work done and work with humans is to interact with them face-to-face rather than following processes. I have experienced many situations where it has been said that certain things are not possible as per the process. But when I talk to people face-to-face, they understand the issue immediately and pick up the work to get it done. The power of interacting with people cannot be underestimated.

The Agile manifesto highlights just that. We should never focus so much on processes and tools. In fact, processes should be used only when required. The focus should be to have interactions with humans, and work with them.

Working software over comprehensive documentation

This manifesto item applies to all sorts of products, not only software products.

After a few decades of Agile application in workplaces, you will be surprised to see the amount of documentation our workplace used to produce. The software development process we used had very heavy information gathering sessions just to understand what the customer wanted. So, a group of business analysts, architects, and managers would sit with the customer and ask them a series of questions, and they would then come up with a written document called the 'user requirements specification' or URS. It was then sent to the customer for verification. The customer would then come back highlighting misunderstandings, and with the corrections required. This process repeated itself a few times. Once approved, the designer would draw the designs on paper and submit them again to the customer for review. The process was repeated until the customer was satisfied, but on paper, not with a working product. This was the traditional way of developing products.

As an example once I inherited an IT service management (ITSM) software product. The software should have been developed and rolled out for 8,000 users in the organization for their work. But the traditional process they followed to develop this software had been started nine months before I inherited that product.

When I took over the development, I received three separate folders each with more than 500 pages. One folder was named 'user requirements specification', another one was the 'solutions design', and the third was the `contract and the project plan'. The product was supposed to be developed by an external consultancy company, hence the contract.

After nine months, and burning little over one million dollars, all they had were those three documents. They did not even have a test version of the product to at least have a look at what it would be like once it was built. When I took over that product, nearly twenty people—from the vendors to the customer—were working on the product but everything they did was on paper: in Excel files and Word documents. There was no working software after nine months and one million dollars' worth of spending.

That was not productive. It was burning money, and the users were frustrated as the current system was slow and outdated. What the customer wanted was a product that they could use instantly. But what they had been focusing on was creating a bunch of documentation instead of working software.

Whether a Product Owner or a manager, a deep understanding of this concept is essential. People tend to use documents to transfer information and to clarify requirements. So, for some people, documents are essential. But this method is very lengthy and complicated. Hence, what we need to do is find a different way to do the same thing because documentation not only produces waste but also delays the product. We need alternatives in order to move away from the document generation process.

Alternatives

There are multiple alternatives to clarify requirements:

Co-create with the customer

Co-creation with the customer is the best way. For example, if you are building a house for a customer, and you make the customer a part of the production team, the entire process will be easier. As the customer is there for the team to ask questions and clarify assumptions, dependencies, etc. It makes the process faster.

Create a prototype

Instead of creating documents, create a prototype. That allows the customer to get an idea of how the product will look and feel in the actual world. Prototypes do not need to be 100 per cent accurate or workable. If they can communicate information more effectively and the customer can make informed decisions, that is more effective and cheaper than producing several documents.

Use technology

We are living in an era where technology is much more complicated than ever before. It is easier and faster, too. For example, some companies have 3D printers. Most Millennials have 3D glasses. There is a new way to bring the virtual into reality with augmented reality. These options are becoming more accessible and cheaper compared to a few years ago. As a result, documents required to clarify requirements can be replaced by such technology.

Customer collaboration over contract negotiation

This Agile manifesto was developed targeting software products. Most cases of product development involve at least two parties. The customer, which is usually another company and, an IT consultancy company which has the capability to develop software products to meet customers' needs. An IT company or IT department of an enterprise or corporate will undertake the work of developing the software in exchange for money. Most of the time, these IT companies are external companies such as agencies or consulting companies. They develop the software for the customer who, in turn, pays the IT company.

In this process, the IT company becomes the service provider while the consuming company/department becomes the client or the customer. To make the process formal and legally binding, a formal contract is created which explains what the IT company will do in terms of scope, timelines and the agreed price to be paid by the customer. This process, which is normally handled by the procurement division, is lengthy and sometimes involves specialized contract writers as well as legal parties. The process is complicated and can be daunting as it involves discussions relating to penalties, service line agreements, contractual obligations, non-disclosure agreements, etc. At the end of the day, the purpose of these contracts is to protect each party.

The entire process goes through several discussions, negotiations and justifications as to why it costs that much money or why it takes that many years or months to develop the product. I have personally been involved in such contract generations because I was working with some consultancy companies. Some of these contractual processes can even go on for two to three months. I would often joke, saying that in 'the time it takes to create the contract and agree to the terms, we can develop a mobile app and release it to be used by the entire world'.

The whole notion of contractual processes is to protect each party. Customers try to protect themselves if something goes wrong. And service providers try to protect themselves if something goes wrong. Hence, they try to be very specific, line-by-line, in detail, because all the time they are thinking about **what if it is not delivered** scenarios. But this is a wasteful process that is built upon suspicion rather than trust. Instead, what we need to do is to build some flexibility to cater to both parties and negotiate what is required to make both parties successful. We need to cultivate **trust and respect for the business models**. That is where partnerships are required instead of lengthy contracts.

As a Product Owner, you will be working with external vendors, suppliers, professional service providers and even team members (external consultants). In that perspective, it is the Product Owner who will be at the receiving end. And because the Product Owner may also be providing services to the customer by developing the product, in that sense, the Product Owner(PO) is at the service provider's receiving end as well. With both these perspectives, what the Product Owner needs to have is flexibility. Instead of heavy contractual processes, the Product Owner needs to spend time building the customers' trust and engaging the external parties as partners in the creative process.

Responding to change over following a plan

Change is everywhere and there is no way to stop it. Once I worked in a global conglomerate. This company experienced huge market growth year by year. As a result, when new customers were acquired, the existing systems had to be upgraded or replaced to cater to the high demand. Within just five years, they replaced their customer relationship management system (CRM) three times. For a user of these CRM systems, that change was huge. Almost every year we had to learn a new system and as a consequence, people responded very negatively. But the truth was that change was required because the company was growing. For example, if the company had 1,000 customers in the first year, in the second year it became 5,000 customers. In the third year, it had 15,000 customers. So the internal systems had to be upgraded to cater for such exponential growth. There was no point in sitting and complaining about it. Changes were happening, and we had to deal with them.

In the traditional way of working, creating plans to get things done is treated important. Once created, the plans need to be followed. But the truth is, changes happen and there is no way to predict what kind of changes we might have to undergo hence cannot exactly follow the plans. The best example is the COVID-19 global pandemic. Did anybody predict the pandemic, or did anyone have a plan to work according to what was happening in the world? What we experienced in 2020 was something not even federal governments had planned for! Hence, what is important is for us to change our plans according to changing situations. We need to accept the changes. We cannot keep on saying that the change was not in the plan.

In the product development process, you as the Product Owner will be part of the process more than anyone else. You will see that things are not moving according to plan. But what is important is an Agile mindset to plan around change and react positively to changes. Because change is the only constant thing.

Agile principles

Agile principles are brain punchers that remind us of the basic concepts of why we do what we do. When we are developing products using the Agile process, we should always remember the Agile principles because those are the foundation stones of the process.

Let's see how these Agile principles relate to the product development process in detail.

The highest priority is to satisfy the customer through early and continuous delivery of valuable software.

Previously, we discussed value delivery to the customer. The sooner the product is developed and delivered to the customer, the more value he/she will get out of the product. Hence, as the Product Owner, your job is to figure out how the product can be delivered to the customer faster. One tested and proved way to do this is through continuous value delivery.

One reason why we cannot deliver a product sooner is that we wait until it is fully complete. Throughout that time the customer has to wait without any product. That is the wait time. For example, let's say it is e-Commerce software which allows the customer to log in to the e-Commerce site and purchase products online. Let's assume there are 50,000 products to sell online.

In product development, we normally try to complete everything, with all payment gateways integrated like Visa, Master, Amex, PayPal, cash on delivery, and all delivery partners like DHL,

FedEx, etc., and all 50,000 products are uploaded. This entire process can sometimes take years. We call this a big bang approach.

Figure 2: Big-bang approach of product development

But a big bang approach is not always required. Instead, as a Product Owner, you can think about a minimum viable product (MVP). That is the minimum number of features a product needs to have to be used by the customers. For example, the e-Commerce solution can have 100 products from a particular category or the most in-demand set of products and cash on delivery or integration with the local post. This is not a full-fledged version but the bare minimum, for the client to see what a fully functional product which can be used by the customer will look like. It may take only a few months to develop such a minimum viable product. Once the MVP is done, then another set of features such as DHL integration and PayPal integration can be done in the next cycle. In this way, with every increment, another set of values is delivered to the customer.

Figure 3: Incremental development with working product at the end of every iteration

It is important for the Product Owner to understand this concept, as you are the person who should make such decisions in the process of developing the product.

Welcome changing requirements, even late in development.

In the traditional method of development, changes are not very welcome. However, changes are inevitable. Customers do change their minds all the time. So regardless of which stage of the development process we are in, we must find a way to accommodate those changes.

The development process needs to be flexible enough so that changes can be accommodated at any time, even at a later stage of the development. Now this is where the Product Owner needs to embrace the Agile frameworks such as Scrum, Large scale Scrum or Scaled Agile Framework (SAFe), etc. Any Agile framework allows enough flexibility to accommodate the changes. Also, this is where the Product Owner needs help from the engineering teams as the architecture of the product needs to be flexible enough to accommodate changes. For example, if you are building a house for the customer and the customer wants to add another bedroom to the house that you have almost finished, the existing architecture of the house should facilitate this new change. To do that, the architecture of the house should have been built to cater for any future changes.

Deliver working software frequently, with a preference for shorter timescales.

This principle goes hand-in-hand with the previous principle of 'welcoming changes even in the later stages of the development cycle'. As we discussed previously, the big bang approach does not work. Hence, the development process should facilitate the incremental value delivery throughout the lifetime of the product. Therefore, instead of having years-long development cycles, Agile is formed around a few weeks' to a few months' development cycles, which we normally call sprints or iterations.

Even though this principle relates to software, it is applicable to business aspects as well. Agile principles are now being applied in business operations, for example, auditing, HR, marketing, and sales apply Agile principles.

Business people and developers must work together daily throughout the project.

I am sure you have had the experience of calling up a bakery or a pastry shop and placing an order for a cake that you want, explaining details regarding the flavor, occasion, colors, and size, etc. Most of the time, we do all this over the phone. And then the baker asks whether we want a message written on the cake or not. One such customer instructed the baker as below:

'Please write "Best Wishes, Suzanne", and underneath that, write, "We will miss you."'

The customer came to the shop the following day to pick up the cake and was shocked to see the cake below:

Figure 4: Misinterpreted requirements (Cakewrecks.com)

In this instance, no doubt the pastry chef was skillful, but the message completely missed the point and as such, the cake was useless. If the customer did not go crazy, he or she must have been a saint!

I have picked the above example from a website called 'Cakewrecks' which showcased hilarious instances where cake orders have gone wrong. This is a very good example to show what happens in product development environments, especially the ones where the production process is outsourced. In fact, we can see this in the case of Best Bank and Super IT, which I referred to in the first chapter.

That is what happens when information is passed on from one person to another and then to another. What the Product Owner understands from the customer may be lost or misinterpreted. And then when the Product Owner communicates the same to the team, they may understand it in a completely different way. Information is messed up in the process of transmission.

The damage is costly. At the end of the day, the customer does not get what he/she wanted. He/she might have to still pay for the product or the waste that the team has produced, and the team may have to start the process all over again.

One of the best ways to resolve this is by co-creation and co-ownership. Customers and other stakeholders including partners, suppliers, Product Owners and the production team should work together. When I say work together, I do not mean they should be connected through meetings, etc. In most of the cases, that is what normally happens. What I mean is for all of them to co-locate and work together as one team.

As the Product Owner, you have the authority to propose and demand the best approach. For example, once I was developing a CRM product and we had two external consultancy companies doing two major feature developments. I insisted they be present at our office, working with our team. They hesitated to say that they preferred to be in their own office. That's when I pulled out a report explaining the number of hours we spend having meetings and still the requirements are not met. I insisted that if they wanted to work on the product, the only way was that they move to our office and integrate with our team or else I would find another supplier. The following week, they co-located with our team, and that made all the difference to the quality of the product.

When we have teams which include everyone, we save time as it increases communication, team bonding and collective understanding. That improves productivity as all these parties work together as one team, sharing the same vision, mission, roadmap, etc.

This approach applies to the Product Owner too. While the team is working together at one place, the Product Owner should not be isolated in a corner office. He/she, too, should be integrated with the team in the same location.

Figure 5: Collaboration between customer and development team

Build projects around motivated individuals. Give them the environment and support they need and trust them to get the job done.

This is one of the reasons why Agile has been very successful, if implemented correctly. The production team is a Product Owner's biggest asset. They know a lot of things the Product Owner may not know. For example, the Product Owner may not know the engineering practices well enough. Hence, he/she must cultivate the style of servant leadership and give autonomy to the team to unleash their potential so that they will actively continue the product development.

Agile takes away command and control leadership. Product Owners who do not give their teams the freedom to develop their own style of work only end up sabotaging the creativity, ownership, and innovation of the team members. It is important that the Product Owner respects the knowledge, background and level of competency of the team. Even the worst performers can be made good performers with the right leadership and coaching. Therefore, the Product Owner should help to build an environment where the team can exercise their creativity without being punished.

The most efficient and effective method of conveying information to, and within, a development team is face-to-face conversation.

In 2008, Forbes conducted a survey by asking 750 business executives whether they like to save money by having meetings remotely or travel to have face-to-face meetings, which is a costly option. Fifty-eight per cent of respondents replied that they liked to travel for face-to-face meetings, irrespective of travel costs (Forbes Insights, 2009).

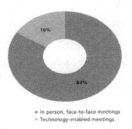

Figure 6: Face-to-face meeting vs. technology-enabled
meetings (Forbes Insights, 2009)

When asked why, they gave many reasons, as shown below.

Figure 7: Executives views on why face-to-face meetings are
better (Forbes Insights, 2009)

If we link team performance to the kind of communication they use, we find that teams with face-to-face communication in co-located environments have a higher and faster performance rate compared to teams where there is no face-to-face communication. Teams with no face-to-face communications, do not bond well; team members do not collaborate with each other and often point fingers when questioned about their part of the work. The result is a delayed product with poor quality.

Speed matters

When we talk about delivering value faster to the customer, we need to reduce the waste in the development process. One of the main delays occurs due to communication gaps. Consider an example. Let's say the Product Owner needs to clarify something with the customer. If the customer is not with the Product Owner in the same location, they have to write emails to each other and wait for the responses. When writing emails, there are always possibilities of misinterpretations and misunderstandings. But if the customer and Product Owner are in the same location, then it is simply a matter of walking across to each other's desks and asking the questions directly. This allows for on the spot two-way communication, which minimizes any communication gaps. This is particularly crucial because when we want to deliver faster and better, every hour, day and week matters; there is no scope for delays.

Working software is the primary measure of progress.

I am sure you are familiar with progress reports. A traditional progress report uses different colors; red, yellow and green, to indicate the status of the production process. If the status is green, it is good as it means things are on time. If it is yellow, Product Owners are a bit worried because it denotes that the project is slightly delayed and not on track. If it is red, it is a serious concern as it is late compared to the planned completion dates. Most of the time, this is how we are used to measuring progress. The issue with this is that this system does not indicate the correct status, because it is progress merely on paper.

Product Feature	Status
Product catalog	◯
PayPal Integration	◯
Delivery Partner integration	●
Shopping cart	⬤

Table 5 : A traditional status report

Sometimes we call these reports 'watermelon reports'. This is because they are red from the inside, but it all looks good and green from the outside. Most of these reports are not a true indication of the right status.

Working software is the only progress report.

If the product is functional, there is no need to show progress reports. Since that is the outcome the customer, stakeholders, Product Owners and the entire team need, all efforts should be directed towards getting the product working, instead of creating status reports.

By showing the working product or in-progress product, all stakeholders can understand how far the development process has gone, and the feedback. Thus, the Product Owner should try to reduce all time-consuming status reports. Instead, the focus should be on showing the functional product.

Agile processes promote sustainable development. The sponsors, developers, and users should be able to maintain a constant pace.

Have you seen a 400-meters race? Some athletes take a lead at the very beginning by using all their techniques, but after 200 or 300 meters, after they have burned all their energy, they slow down and finish the race last. In contrast, runners who have a very slow start but maintain a steady pace throughout the race manage not only to finish but more often to win the race. Hence, what is important is to keep up a sustainable and constant pace.

This is what is required in the development process as well. Most of the time, Product Owners put pressure on the team to do more and more. I have seen people work eighteen hours or seven days a week. That has never produced good quality products. Such continuous work—even though it shows constant work—guarantees a few setbacks:

It makes people fatigued, mechanical, angry, and emotional.

The above reasons make people demotivated. Even if they want to, they do not have any energy left to think properly and produce innovative, good quality products.

Hence, poor quality products are produced, which leads to customers' dissatisfaction.

Agile promotes self-organization and sustainability. The team can decide on their own capacity, since they must have a healthy work style. Agile operates on a pull system rather than a push system, encouraging teams to figure out their own capacity and be accountable for what they have committed to. In my experience, this has always worked very well.

Push vs pull system

Most traditional product/project teams operate as push systems. That means the managers push the team to work and the team does that work. Managers want the team to do a certain amount of work even when the team says they cannot do that much. As an example, when a software engineer says a certain web page development needs roughly two days, managers challenge that and say 'you have to do that in four hours'. In such cases, team members' knowledge is thrown into the gutter and managers force them to do the work in a very narrow timeframe. As a result, team members work day and night to complete the work within the time assigned by the managers, which is not sustainable.

Instead of pushing work, Agile tries to maintain sustainability by creating a pull system. What does this mean? Agile has created a few practices for building a pull system, and these include the team deciding its own capacity or the workload it can take on regularly. This is normally known as velocity. In the pull system, the team pulls work based on the priorities set by the customer or Product Owner. This way, the customer gets the anticipated value, yet the team does not experience a burn out.

Continuous attention to technical excellence and good design enhances agility.

Simple can be harder than complex.

You have to work hard to get your thinking clean to make it simple.   **Steve Jobs**

I once visited one of my friends in Bangalore, India. He and his family lived on the sixth floor of a high-rise apartment complex. Since it was an old building, they did not have an elevator, just stairs. Every time they wanted something from outside, they had to climb down the stairs, and then climb back up again. That means they had to plan better about when to go out and for what. Meanwhile, they had found a clever way of transporting some items like fish, vegetables, and the like from the ground floor to the sixth floor.

A simple system that serves the purpose

In India, it is common for fishmongers and vegetable sellers to go from door-to-door with fresh produce. They mount everything on a bicycle and go to each house, shouting out things they are selling. Housewives who need those supplies come to the bicycle to select the goods they want and pay the seller on the spot. This means that my friends who were living in this high-rise had to head downstairs every time they wanted to buy something.

The clever system they had found involved tying a rope to a plastic basket, which they would send down when the fishmonger or vegetable seller came. They would yell what they wanted from the sixth floor, and the seller would weigh it and put it into the basket. My friend's wife would then pull up the rope and it would bring up the basket with the supplies. She would then empty the basket, put in the money, and send down the basket again. Everyone in such apartment complexes was doing the same. This is a simple system, but it served the purpose well.

Sometimes what we need are very simple systems.

Applying this principle to the products we design tells us that sometimes what we need are very simple systems. Therefore, we must invest our time and effort into building simple yet powerful designs with the potential to accommodate future changes.

We may have seen engineering teams trying to build complex designs meant to solve simple problems. By all means, building good designs is smart, but we have to keep asking the question: Is there a way to simplify this? This is a challenge for engineers and technical teams. In software engineering, after taking this into account, we have seen pioneer architectural designs, like micro-services emerging, Similarly, in a problem-solving environment, we need to find ways to simplify the design and build more fluid systems, so that future changes can be easily accommodated.

Simplicity, the art of minimizing the amount of unnecessary work, is essential.

Unused product features

According to research done by the Standish Group, only 20 per cent of the features of custom-developed applications are used. That means 80 per cent of features are rarely or hardly used. This is pretty much aligned with what I have experienced in product development. We spend more time and effort building features which add hardly any value to the customer. Sometimes, customers demand some features thinking they might be necessary, but they do not state any rationale behind why those features might be required, let alone how much value those particular features would deliver

Figure 8: Software product feature usage (Standish group, 2015)

Let's take an example. Go to Microsoft Word which you probably use a lot. Look at how many menu items you have used. Most of the time the list will include: creating a new document, saving, opening, printing, spell and grammar check etc. But now look at how many other menu items are available in MS-word. There are certainly some items you have never used. That simply demonstrates that products do have lots of features which may not be absolute must-haves. This is proven by the research done by the Standish group. As per the report, 50% of features in software is hardly used.

That is why we need to think twice before we start the process of building anything. We need to consider carefully how much these processes cost in time and money.

Economical way

Building any product or product feature takes time, money, and effort. After spending so much effort, if the product or the feature created does not deliver any value, then the effort ends up being a sheer waste. That money could have been spent to generate some other product of value. It is, therefore, important to prioritize product features before we commit to spending more money and time on them.

Customers who want only the most important product features get their value more quickly. They also get to pay only for what they need instead of spending money on less sellable product features or product features they hardly use.

From the viewpoint of the development team, it allows them to spend their efforts on the most important product features, and they are more motivated to solve the problems most important to the customers.

Agile practices

Agile has a few practices that promote this principle, including the creation of product backlog, product backlog prioritization based on value, writing user stories, and so on. These practices are helpful when it comes to delivering economic value to the customer and utilizing the best efforts of the team.

The best architectures, requirements, and designs emerge from self-organizing teams.

You should not hire smart people and tell them what to do.

Steve Jobs

At the beginning of my career, I worked as a software engineer. After five years of working in a reputed software company, I joined another company. I was part of a twenty-member team under one team leader. At that time, there were no Agile concepts, hence we were all working in the traditional style where the team leader assigns the team members their work.

I became very frustrated when my manager started micro-managing me and telling me how I should do my work. Once we finished writing the code and testing it, he asked us to assemble at his desk, where he went through all of our codes and started re-writing them as he pointed out mistakes. From the time he called us to his desk around 4.30 p.m., we could not leave the office until around 7 p.m. when he completed re-writing our codes. Each of us had to go through that process, and it was not a good experience to see this team leader erase our code and re-write it the way he wanted it. When he kept doing that repeatedly, he reminded us of how crappy our code-writing was, and how brilliantly he could write it. The organization did not have any coding standards, therefore each of us had done what we were used to. His micro-management and ill-treatment affected each of us very negatively. It was demotivating.

We did not warrant any lectures on how crappy our work was, but we remained open-minded about what we should do to improve. Nevertheless, the way the team leader went about correcting us, diminished our creativity and spirit. I left the company within six weeks, and the rest of my colleagues followed. After just a few years, that company went bankrupt. This experience has convinced me that he was the kind of boss I do not want to ever work with again in my life.

Our workspace has transformed drastically during the last twenty years. We no longer have corner offices for the managers; instead they sit with the teams. We do not have command and control managers. Instead, we have servant leaders. We have embraced Agile; leaders do listen to employees to make informed decisions.

Autonomy and self-organized teams

As a Product Owner, you possess a certain amount of authority. But I have seen sometimes this authority being wrongly used, for example, when the Product Owner puts pressure on teams and tells them what to do. That is not the best way of getting efficient outcomes from the team.

Instead, let's try to believe that the team can organize themselves around their capabilities. One person has one capability, which another person does not have. Hence, when we have a team of ten people, they together bring a very diverse yet powerful combination of skills and capabilities to the production site. That is, only if the Product Owner lets them experiment with their skills. What the Product Owner needs to do is to make the environment more free and collaborative by encouraging the team to fail and learn from their mistakes.

I recall one of the projects I did with a global mining company. They wanted to apply the Agile way of working, and we started to pilot with multiple countries and divisions. One of the product teams consisted of geologists, geophysicists, and reservoir engineers. The product they were working on was to determine where to drill for an oil well in back waters. The project involved a series of varied data point calculations and predictive analytics. Although the team used their internal tools as expected, they also went ahead and collected data from other regional data centers. No one, not even the senior manager or Product Owner, had asked them to do this. But they went ahead and did it on their own initiative. That information blew everyone's mind because the resultant suggestions that came up were backed by data that no one had ever used and analyzed. This is because previously senior managers used to tell teams what to do and how to do it, the team's thinking ability was limited to only what the managers told them.

However, this time around, as part of Agile transformation, senior managers were not allowed to interfere with their teams by giving orders, and instead, teams were given full autonomy and accountability. That specific team made managers realize that teams are indeed capable of doing things in the best way possible. And most of the time, they are better than managers.

This is applicable to you, too, as a Product Owner. What you need to do is to make the team accountable and hand over the ownership of the product to them. It is not just the Product Owner's product; it is the product of the team, too. So, in the production process, the team should be allowed to organize themselves in a way that they think best.

At regular intervals, the team reflects on how to become more effective, then fine-tunes and adjusts its behavior accordingly.

Figure 9: Resisting continuous improvement

In one of the SAFe Agile trainings I conducted, a senior leader aired his view about Agile. After going through one day of training, he said: 'This is the same old shit with a new name.'

He was correct. Most of us do the same things under a new name or brand. The core things we do or the way we work never change. Only the name changes. If we continue with useless practices from the traditional development process, Agile is going to be 'the same old shit'.

However, if we care to have a deep understanding of the Agile manifesto and principles, then things will be different. The underlying philosophy of Agile is to rule out the inefficient practices of the traditional way of developing products. That is why continuous improvement and adaptation is mandatory for any Agile project. In every set-up, some things work and some do not. For the organization to run profitably, it must work on continuous improvements. That is what Agile does: allows for continuous improvement.

This means that everyone associated with the product, not just the Product Owner or team manager, but also the team, regularly analyzes what is working and what is not.

Ownership of improvement and making things better

All organizations strive for continuous improvement. But very rarely are these changes or improvements successful. The reason being that these changes are suggested by senior leadership and implemented at the operational level. The senior leadership does not have practical insights into what is going wrong, nor does the operational staff understand what change is being suggested and why. Hence, the team feels rejected, and does not comply. The result of such a change is waste of money, time, and effort; in short, a total failure. On the contrary, Agile gives the ownership of improvement to the team. They are the people who do the work on the ground level, so they decide whether something works for the team or not. If something is not working, then they are the ones who should come up with a plan to improve upon it.

The Product Owner should be open to the team's ideas for improvement. Since they are also part of the team, they are an equal contributor to the overall working of it. At times it may be necessary to adapt to the suggestions that the team makes, even if it means changing their style of working. For example, the team may say: 'Our product feature prioritization is not clear; priorities have changed frequently. This is not helping us as we have to keep changing our focus. Can we make prioritization clear before we start the work?'

A statement like this may surprise the Product Owner, because he/she might be under the impression that he/she is doing things right and everything is clear. But instead of defending himself/herself, Product Owner should understand that his/her instructions **are not clear to the team.** So, Product Owner needs to ask himself/herself the question: How can we make prioritization clear? This will begin the process of ideation and the team members will chip in with ideas on how to improve. As a result, everybody has the ownership of making things better. And this is what makes Agile unique.

The relationship between Agile and product development

We know that products need to deliver a unique value to the customer within a small timeframe. To be profitable to the customer as well as to the production organization, the product development process needs to produce only the product, and not waste. Agile as a methodology focuses on delivering value to the customer, faster and better. The foundation of Agile is to produce maximum value by reducing waste. Agile provides a new way of working to deliver value faster.

Summary

The traditional product development method, for software or other products, has caused more harm than good. The phase-by-phase approach lengthens the development process and requires customers to wait till everything is done. But during that waiting period, lots of things might change that could cause the customer to demand modifications and excessive rework. This is not very effective, productive or sustainable. That is why a new, better way is required, in fact, is essential.

As per research and case studies, Agile is a much better way to develop a product. Its iterative development helps to deliver incremental value to the customer, reducing the waiting time and making it easier to react to changes required by the customer. This is a much more flexible and engaging way to deliver true value to the customer.

References

Cakewrecks, 2020, Retrieved from https://www.cakewrecks.com/

Chaos Report, 2015, The Standish Group International

Manifesto for Agile Software Development, 2001, retrieved from https://agilemanifesto.org/

Principles behind the Agile Manifesto, 2001, retrieved from https://agilemanifesto.org/

CHAPTER 2
AGILE ORGANIZATION

D eveloping a product requires highly skilled people working together towards one goal: to deliver a valued product to the customer and earn a return on investment from that product. Doing this over a period of time without losing motivation is a rather complex matter.

To achieve this goal, product development should be thought of as a small enterprise. It is much more than a few people forming a group and working on a day-to-day basis.

One can take inspiration and ideas for this from already set-up models, such as Galbraith's star model.

This is widely used in business organizational set-ups. Galbraith's star model explains the essential components any business needs to consider while setting up. Let us discuss the components of the star model in some detail.

Galbraith's star model

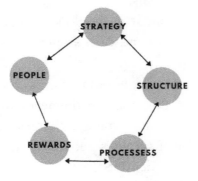

Figure 10: Galbraith's star model

This model comes into the picture when we study organizational theories. How should an organization be set up? What is needed to deliver an organization's goal?

Organizational design and theories are in themselves a separate and lengthier subject. But the concept of an organization is relevant to product development because product development itself is an organization. There are many components which need to work together to develop a product over a period of time.

According to this model, there are five main components to setting up an organization: Strategy, structure, process, rewards and people. Let's examine these components individually, in detail.

Strategy

Strategy defines the framework for decision-making. What kind of business are we in? What products are we offering? Which customer segment are we partnered with? What are our values? How do we earn money? What things do we do? And what don't we do? Who are our partners? Who are our suppliers? Strategy provides a framework to answer these questions and hence to make necessary decisions. When the strategy is clear, it is relatively easy to focus on the way forward and to stop derailments.

Strategy consists of three main components: vision, strategic themes and strategic goals. Every organization's strategy is structured around a vision. It is developed further by dividing it into many strategic themes and each strategic theme is developed using strategic goals.

When applying this to the product organization, chances are this product is part of the strategic theme of the organizational strategy. It is likely that these strategic themes have already been discussed and the product specifics needed to address the strategic theme have already been identified. This simply means that when you start product development in your production unit, those same strategic themes need to be replicated. Hence, it is always a good idea to check with your seniors on the specific strategic theme.

We will discuss these strategic themes in detail in the following chapters.

Structure

How should the product organization be structured? What functions should the product organization have? How should these different functions be networked or linked?

Organizational structure is very important in any organization. It decides the work culture of the organization as well as determining how things are done. Structure also determines who is authorized to make a decision and how those decisions should be executed and by whom.

Some structures are hierarchical where the top management makes decisions while the bottom layers are expected to execute those decisions. Some structures are flat where everyone in the organization has the same decision-making power. In these flatter organizations there are fewer intermediate layers, hence some feel the decision-making is faster. However, both structures do have pros and cons, and therefore some organizations follow a hybrid approach. The new way of working proposes, and challenges us to come up with, new structures in the organizational set-up. Agile promotes self-organization and autonomy. Hence, it needs to have a flat or less hierarchical structure.

Having the right structure from the beginning is essential to the success of the product. This is where the Agile organizational structure comes into the picture. In comparison, Agile provides multiple ways to structure these different functions. For example, Agile teams are cross-functional. Multi-disciplinary members come together as one unit and work as a team rather than spread through various functions.

Process

How is the organization going to operate? What are the functions of each department? What are the terms that team members will agree on, when working together? What steps are to be followed to get a certain thing done? These are the questions answered by the process. Processes define what to do and what not to do to reach a certain goal. These are like agreements between different units of operations. Although processes are required, a heavy-duty process creates delays, as we have discussed in the previous chapter. Hence, the right balance of processes is important in any organization.

Rewards

Do you remember when you heard your parents clapping the first time you sang a song in public? Or your teacher's comments on your notebook saying 'A+' or 'Very Good'? Such gestures are very important and necessary to motivate the team to keep moving forward. It is a way of letting them know that their work is being appreciated and to reassure them that they are on the right track. That is why reward structures are a very integral part of any organization.

Even though the reward structure is an integral component of any work process, most organizations forget about it. When we talk about organizations, it is important to talk about rewards because that brings in a holistic approach to the work culture of an organization.

At the same time, the reward structure should be able to motivate people at difficult times as well. Also, not everybody is motivated in the same manner. While a small 'Thank you' note will lift one person's spirits, for another person, it may be a useless set of words. The right reward structure can lift a team while the wrong one can completely derail them.

The reward structure is a complicated matter, but has a particularly important role in any organizational structure, including the production environment. Hence, if you are starting the product from scratch, it is a good idea to discuss the reward structure of the product development team right at the beginning.

And if you are inheriting a product, then it is a good idea to review the existing reward structure or establish a new one if there is not one in place.

People

Who are the people you want in your team? What skill level do they need? What kind of leadership are you expecting from them? What kind of experience level and background do they need to have? What level of motivation do they need? What is the necessary diversity level? All these things should be considered at the beginning of any product set-up. When these criteria are clear at the beginning, it helps the Product Owner(PO) to reduce recruitment delays and people development efforts as there will be no time wasted on culturally unsuitable candidates or dealing with people issues when the work begins. It is not that no issues will arise once the project starts, but the more issues that are dealt with at the beginning, the better equipped a Product Owner(PO) is to tackle new issues as they arise.

Star model and product organization

I have discussed the five-star model in a product environmental set-up to invite you to think differently and think about the big picture. Developing a product is not a one month or two month job. A product could be the main revenue source or the reason why an organization exists.

Thus, setting up the product development organization in the right manner is as important as starting to develop a product. Through the star model, I would like you to understand the holistic approach to setting up product organization. Having an understanding of this will help you to relate to how the Agile product development set-up is structured, why certain practices are important, and how certain processes help in the production process. In the next chapter, we will examine how Agile can be used to structure the product organization.

How Agile teams are organized

In this section we will discuss how a production team is organized using Agile. Luckily, Agile provides many ways to organize and even to scale up a product. It also provides multiple frameworks that create different organizational structures. However, it all depends on various factors like the nature of the product you are developing, the complexity of it, the structure of the enterprise, maturity of the organization, etc. An enterprise Agile coach is one of the best sources of information to get more details about these Agile frameworks.

The nucleus of the product development process

An Agile product team is the nucleus of any product organization. Getting this team right will solve half the problems. When structured properly, an Agile team is a power pack. But if structured wrongly, it will not be any different from the old school of organization. Let's see how an Agile team is structured.

Agile/product team

A cross-functional Agile team is a power pack. They are the people who create raw materials, product design, and assemble parts to produce the product. Starting right from product inception to design and then to production and after sales support, an Agile team takes complete ownership of the entire product life cycle.

Normally, an Agile team consists of seven to eleven team members including the Scrum Master (Agile process owner), Product Owner, as well as content producers, user experience designers, software engineers, business analysts and operational team members.

There is a reason why the Agile team is small but cross-functional. As you may have experienced in bigger organizations, when we deal with a larger number of people, there are hierarchies and we lose the flexibility and responsiveness of the team.

For example, let's assume that you want to go on a holiday. You decide that only close family—your mother, father, wife and your two children—should go together. Since it is your immediate family members and you have a close communication network with them, it will be easy to organize. But if you want to include extended family as well—your wife's mother's side, father's side, your siblings and their family members, cousins and their family members, etc.— I can guarantee that you will never go on that holiday. This is because the more people involved, the more complexity it adds to the situation. Coming to an agreement on any issue will be very time consuming, and therefore less effective.

That is why Agile teams are very small in terms of numbers. That gives the transparency required to be flexible. Which means that Agile teams can have a face-to-face conversation with each other and decide very quickly in which direction they should move forward. That is how self-organization and autonomy are increased in an Agile team.

Power of small teams

The power of a small team cannot be underestimated. For example, the Apple iMovie product was developed by three team members. Apple's iPhoto was created by only five people. Instagram, at the time of being acquired by Facebook, was developed by thirteen people, while Spotify was developed by eight people. This is a shockingly small number, especially for larger organizations who are used to having an army of people to develop products.

I have personally experienced this concept throughout my career while working with small and large organizations. A streaming product I worked on is one of the best examples. It was a start-up and the streaming product we developed was used by television channels across Australia, Canada, and the UK. If you are in any of these countries, you might be already using the product we developed every time you stream popular television shows via your mobile device. This streaming solution was developed by seven people within just six months. But we were fully Agile. We applied every Agile manifesto item. I don't recall writing any contracts with any of the TV channels; we also did not have any URS, etc., and we applied every Agile principle I have discussed previously. A big product was developed by a very small team.

In contrast, I have worked with larger organizations where thousands of employees developed different types of products. Some of those products included several hundreds of people. They were managed using traditional project management methodologies, which we call 'Waterfall', and the results were delayed product launches. Some product launches took years to complete. Some products had to be scrapped because by the time they were ready to be marketed, customers had already found a different product.

That is the reason all Agile frameworks such as Scrum, Large Scale Scrum, Scaled Agile Framework recommend having seven to eleven people in a nucleus Agile team. When the product is complex, it may need many such teams, but the atomic team always needs to be small and cross-functional to get the best results. Such an atomic team has three integral roles, as explained below.

Figure 11: Agile team

Scrum Master

A Scrum Master is the steward of the Agile process. He/she plays a key role in the team and has a servant leadership position. He/she knows everything about the Agile process and can guide the team and the Product Owner in the right direction in terms of agile practices. The Scrum Master coaches and guides the Product Owner through tough situations in the product development process such as how to create the product backlog, how the features should be prioritized, etc.

The Scrum Master makes sure the team follows the plan and Agile practices. He/she is the Product Owner's partner in the product development process. Without his/her support and guidance, Agile cannot be properly implemented.

Agile team

The Agile team consists of cross-functional team members, excluding the Scrum Master and the Product Owner. They operate on their own, and can decide on the best way to develop the product. For example, they know how to write the code, how to test according to the industry standards, etc. They are experts in the work that they do.

They meet regularly because they are mostly co-located. They collaborate, but sometimes they may have conflicts as well which they will figure out how to navigate. The Product Owner and Scrum Master should not micro-manage the team.

As a Product Owner, you should know how to work with the team. The most important Agile mindset that the Product Owner needs to develop and understand is that the team doesn't work for the Product Owner. Rather, they work with the Product Owner. Each of them is extremely skilled and capable, and they will give their full capacity to the process only if you allow them to. What is required is to respect the knowledge they have. That will bring out the best in them, which will in turn benefit the product.

The Product Owner(PO)'s job is to provide the team with the product vision, goals of the product, connections with the stakeholders, prioritization of the product features, what criteria are required by the Product Owner to accept the work they do or the product features, etc.

In the development process, the team will come across a lot of details that might lead them to many questions. Hence, the Product Owner's availability is important for the team. The Product Owner should develop an environment where the team feels safe to ask questions. The Product Owner needs to understand that the team will sometimes fail; that without failing, the product cannot be developed. Hence, failures should be treated as an integral part of the product success.

Product Owner

The Product Owner has multiple responsibilities within the Agile team. The main responsibility is making sound decisions on the product features, value creation and prioritization of delivery. Seamless communication with the team and assurance of delivery on time and quality are an important part of the Product Owner's job.

Team of Agile teams

A small team is more than enough to develop a small product. Most of the time, this team will be developing the core product. However, other parallel functions may be required for the product launch in the market or for the customer.

For example, let's say there is a B2C e-Commerce solution. The nucleus Agile team is accountable for developing the e-Commerce software, which is a website and a mobile app. But the product has other sub-products as well. For example, a company cannot sell a product only by having a good website or mobile apps. To sell the products, the raw material needs to be purchased from the suppliers, it needs to be sent to the warehouse to store, then the items need to be packaged, the packaging needs to have company logos which need to be printed by a third-party printer. Then if the products are required to be sold in the international market, they need to be marketed. So, a series of functions are needed parallel to the e-commerce and app development.

These other functions also can be organized following the same Agile principles. This means another Agile team working parallel to the first team has to be created.

Figure 12: Parallel teams

Depending on the complexity and the scale of the product, a number of such teams will be required to develop a complete, ready-to-market product.

However, one pitfall to avoid is to combine all the teams into one large team. Such teams will lose agility and the ability for self-organization. Hence, Agile teams need to be organized into smaller teams, which share the same product vision.

Summary

As you have seen in this chapter, it is essential that the team is structured in the right manner to support the product development. Just having a team with Agile practices integrated and using the Agile method, is not enough. It is necessary to understand what skills and people are needed, and to set up the operating structure and reward structure correctly so that product development is sustainable, productive and enjoyable for all parties involved. As a Product Owner you must think about all this before you dive into the ownership of a product.

References

GALBRAITH, J. 2014, Designing Organizations, Strategy, Structure, and Process at the Business Unit and Enterprise Levels, SBN: 978-1-118-40995-4

CHAPTER 3
AGILE PRODUCT DEVELOPMENT PROCESS

P roduct development using Agile is remarkably successful thanks to the radical way it has been organized, structured and the enforced practices. These practices have been applied and used for nearly two decades now and we see their success compared to non-Agile practices. Hence, we urge product development to follow the same practices as they always yield good results when applied properly.

At the team level, the Agile process is structured around artifacts, agile cadence and ceremonies. The figure below illustrates the product development process which uses Scrum as the agile methodology.

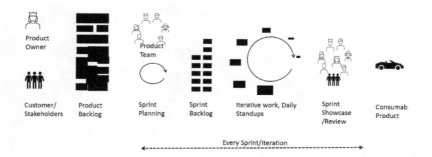

Figure 13: Product development process using Agile

An Agile team is the main component of the production set-up. The Product Owner as the voice of the customer, decides the product development priorities and the decision-making in terms of the priorities. The Product Owner keeps track of everything to be developed for the product in a basket called 'product backlog'.

The Scrum Master guides the team and the Product Owner on the Agile process which should be followed. The entire product development is divided into iterations called 'sprints'. A sprint is a short duration like two to three weeks.

Throughout the sprint, the team follows a rhythm called a cadence. This cadence consists of sprint planning, daily standups, backlog planning, sprint showcase or review and sprint retrospective. When the two weeks finish then the cycle begins again to develop another prioritized product subset. When there is a satisfactory product subset, the team and the Product Owner decide to release it to the customer. Through this disciplined process items in the backlog will be materialized as the usable product.

In a nutshell, this is how the Agile organization can be used to develop products faster and better. Let's examine the components of this set-up in detail in the next section.

Product backlog

Product backlog refers to the list of product features which need to be developed, modified, or removed. Typically, it is everything to be done to develop the product as a consumable unit. These product features consist of technical, non-technical, operational, and business features of the product. The notion is, if it is not in the product backlog, it is not going to be developed hence it will not be in the product. However, it does not mean that everything in the product backlog is going to be developed either. Therefore prioritization is necessary to decide if the product features in the backlog are developed or not. So the guiding mechanism to decide the prioritization is the return on investment.

The contents of the product backlog may vary in size. There will be product features with clear details on how they should look or how they should function. But there will be items with fewer details or just at the idea level. As an example, making an e-Commerce website in different languages like in Hindi, Dutch, Arabic and French are at a high level. It is just an idea. Details on how to do it and the complexities associated with that concept are not available at that moment. Hence product backlog will consist of items with high level, less detailed items as well as low level, detailed items.

Where do these product features come from? They originate from market research, customer requests, stakeholder feedback, team feedback, improvement ideas or issues and bugs in the existing product.

What happens to the contents of the backlog?

Contents in the backlog go through a series of exercises to understand the context, validations, and to analyze the return on investment (ROI). Based on ROI, all backlog items will be ranked in order of priority. The Product Owner organizes the product backlog to display the priority items on the top. The items with the highest priority will be selected for immediate development. That means eventually the product backlog items with a high priority will be made real as a consumable product feature.

The product backlog is a live repository. It is like a warehouse which gets replenished all the time with new items. Items in the product backlog will get emptied and at the same time products will start to flow to the product backlog during the entire life of the product.

Sprint backlog

A sprint is a short duration; generally, one to four weeks of development. The list of highest prioritized items from the backlog is selected to develop in the next sprint. This list of items is known as the sprint backlog. So, it is a subset of a backlog only for the duration of the sprint.

Depending on the priority the Product Owner has set and

the capacity the team has within the sprint, the team will select the items from the backlog to fit the sprint capacity. Once selected, the Agile team will focus on getting the work done during the sprint and there should not be more product features added to the 'sprint backlog' during the sprint cycle.

The team will break down the product features into something called 'user stories' and 'tasks' and distribute them among themselves as per the skills required to develop that user story. However, at the end of the day, the Product Owner has the authority to accept or reject the user stories developed by them. Hence the Product Owner must provide the necessary criteria to be met for the user stories to be accepted. This is known as 'acceptance criteria'.

However, this does not mean that everything in the sprint backlog will be completed by the end of the sprint. The intention is to complete the sprint backlog. However, if the team encounters problems or dependencies beyond their capabilities, then the work is not going to be finished within the sprint duration. That is when they need the Product Owner and Scrum Master's help. When they inform the Product Owner of these blockers or hurdles, the Product Owner should help them by offering the necessary support so that they can still complete all the items in the sprint backlog.

Agile team cadence

Cadence defines the rhythm of the team. This rhythm consists of a few events and practices to ensure the team meets its sprint goal (completing the sprint backlog). These events are pretty much well defined in all Agile frameworks. These events are well tested and retested to a level to say 'this is how it should be done'. Below is an explanation of the cadence emphasizing the role of the Product Owner and the distinct responsibilities of the Product Owner(PO).

Sprint/Iteration

A sprint or iteration is a development cycle. It can be one week, two weeks, three weeks, or four weeks. Anything below or above has proven less successful and defeated the purpose of iterative development. The purpose of iteration is to lockdown the scope for the sprint duration and deliver the sprint scope. Statistics demonstrate that two-week sprints are more successful than one-, three- or four-week sprints. Two-week sprints give enough time to analyze, develop, test, and get customer feedback before new work is taken up.

During the sprint duration, the team attends a few events as explained below.

Time	Day									
	Monday	Tuesday	Wednesday	Thursday	Friday	Monday	Tuesday	Wednesday	Thursday	Friday
9.30 AM - 10 AM			standup	standup	standup	standup	standup	standup	standup	standup
10.00 AM - 11 AM										
11.00 AM - 12 noon		Sprint Planning								
12.00 - 1.00 PM	showcase and Lunch									
1.00 PM - 2 PM										
2PM AM - 3 PM						Backlog Grooming				
3 PM - 4 PM	Retrospective									
4 PM - 5PM										

Figure 14: Agile cadence

Sprint planning

Sprint planning is an essential and critical event of any Agile team. During the sprint planning, the team decides what they are going to develop (scope), how to develop it, and the amount they can develop. It is a commitment between the Product Owner and the development team during the sprint. Sprint planning is a scoping session for the duration of the sprint.

Sprint planning normally is a four-hour session for two-week sprints. All team members, the Scrum Master and the Product

Owner meet face-to-face to discuss what product features need to be developed within the next two weeks.

During sprint planning, the team needs to achieve the following:

- Define the sprint goal (i.e., the home page of an e-Commerce website or chatbot for a customer support function)

- Prioritize a list of product features for achieving the sprint goal (i.e., a chatbot)

- Identify the user stories required as per the product features and the sprint goal

- Gain a clear understanding of the complexities and interdependencies, as well as a high-level plan of how they might be solved (not solutions)

- Estimate the user stories using the measurements guided by the Scrum Master

- Identify what is committable and what is not committable as per the team velocity

- Clarify the user story acceptance criteria

- Commit to the sprint scope.

The Product Owner's involvement in this session is extremely critical. The team asks many questions to clarify the acceptance criteria and the Product Owner needs to respond to those questions. It is possible even the Product Owner may not have clear answers so together the team should discuss the acceptance criteria and agree with the Product Owner. When the sprint planning session is a constructive discussion, the Product Owner, as well as the other team members, can get a clear understanding on where they are in terms of understanding and the complexity of the user story or the product feature.

Hence the Product Owner must prepare the details before starting the sprint planning session. The backlog grooming session is that preparation time.

Backlog planning/grooming

The backlog planning or grooming session happens in the middle of every sprint. It is just a preparation for the upcoming sprints. The product backlog should be always up to date with the right level of details and priorities so that in the next sprint the most critical and urgent work will be dealt with.

The product backlog is a live container. It keeps getting new product features from everyone and everywhere. These new items come from the Product Owner's ideas or stakeholders or the team or the users who are using the product at that moment. Some of the items need immediate actions. As an example, if a bug or defect has been reported by the users, then it needs to be solved immediately. If there is a new government regulatory requirement which impacts the product, this needs immediate action. If one of the supplier's product uses (such as a delivery partner) goes bankrupt, the Product Owner needs to take immediate action to find an alternative and integrate with the new alternatives. These new items change the existing priorities or plan the Product Owner has developed. The Product Owner probably needs to talk to a lot of people, stakeholders, other business divisions etc. for details.

The Product Owner may need to get other people involved during this session such as the chief architect, customer, SMEs of other business divisions etc. As an example, if there is a change to the regulatory requirements, the Product Owner needs the regulatory SME or the legal division in this session. So, the Product Owner needs to get them to attend this session in order to extract the right level of details to make informed decisions, which ultimately go into the backlog.

Standup

Standup is just a fifteen-minute session which happens every day. It includes all the team members, the Product Owner and Scrum Master. This daily briefing ensures everyone in the team understands where they stand in terms of achieving the sprint goal commitments.

It is a time-boxed event, that means it needs to start on time and finish on time. Each team member updates the others in the team by providing three main, important pieces of information. These are: what they were working on the previous day, and the status of it, in terms of it is finished, ready for the next step; what they are going to work on today; and if they face any roadblocks achieving what they have committed to doing. Stand up should not be misunderstood as a detailed status update meeting with long discussions, and presentations. It is short, enough for each member to provide an update on the status of their work.

Standup is an essential session for the Product Owner as it will give him/her an idea as to whether the team is on track to deliver what they have committed to. That information can be used to report on progress to other stakeholders. Also, the session will help the Product Owner to understand if the team reveals some dependencies or issues which stop them doing their work. This is the time to jump starlight and help them with the necessary information or decisions or link them with the right people/ stakeholders to unblock the roadblocks.

During the standup, the team will update the Kanban wall indicating where their user story is in the flow. If the team uses a digital tool like Jira or other software, they will update the same. This should be more than enough for the Product Owner and Scrum Master to understand the progress of the user stories.

Showcase/sprint review

Showcase happens at the end of the sprint. Showcase or sprint review helps to get customer feedback as soon as a few user stories or features are developed at the end of the sprint. It is one of the best ways to address many issues we normally see in product development environments.

Customers do not directly engage with the product, so they have no idea what the product looks like until it is developed.

Stakeholders who are contributing to the product also have no idea because they don't directly interact with the development team.

End users/stakeholders have questions on why and how certain product features are prioritized over other desired features.

Since showcase engages them at very regular intervals, as soon as the sprint finishes, they have the option of seeing the newly developed features and to tell the team if they like them or not.

The Product Owner can even try out the product features developed in the showcase. I remember once when we were developing a mobile app for a corporate customer, at the end of the sprint the team asked all of us to bring our mobile phones to the sprint showcase. During the session, they asked us to download the mobile app from the app store or Google store and sign up. That is the best way to showcase the product, much better than status reports. We were happy to download it. Not that it worked the way it was intended as some people were not able to connect to Wifi etc., but those issues provided instant feedback to the team on the real issues associated with the product features.

Retrospective

Agile takes continuous improvement seriously. No process can be optimized if it is not improved regularly. Agile teams review their process at regular intervals (i.e., in every sprint), so these reviews, normally referred to as retrospectives, are critical and should take place at the end of every sprint, without fail.

Teams look back on the process they followed to determine what worked for them and what did not. If something has worked, then they can decide to continue the same way in the next sprint too, but if it hasn't, then they can discuss why it failed. This is normally the nature of a sprint retrospective.

In the process of developing a sustainable product, this retrospective is very important because the process needs improvement and fine-tuning from time to time. Hence, Agile teams will do the following.

Conduct the retrospectives at regular intervals:

Sprint showcase is at the end of every sprint. It is a mandatory event. One common pattern we identify from high performing scrum teams is that they never skip retrospectives. It is a Scrum Master's job to convince the team to conduct the retrospective and ensure it takes place. The Product Owner also should insist and participate in the sprint retrospectives as Product Owners are part of the team.

Create a safe and trusting environment:

The retrospective is the team's event. This is the event to correct things. It is the event in which should be honest about the process they are following. Team members should be able to speak freely in the retrospective. Team members should be able to criticize their process/behaviors and their opinions/ideas should not be judged. In this context they will be honest in giving their feedback to make the process better.

The Product Owner and the Scrum Master should respect the discussion points. As an example, sometimes the team will say things like 'Acceptance criteria is not that clear', 'we are pivoting too much' or something similar. For better results, the Product Owner needs to be open-minded and work with the team to fix the areas that are not working.

Participate actively:

Everyone's opinions and ideas matter. Hence, listen to them very carefully. What they say may be a complete shock to the Product Owner. Also, listen to unspoken words. Listen to the body language of the team. Are they comfortable sharing their ideas or concerns in front of a Product Owner? If the Product Owner feels otherwise, the Product Owner should discuss this with the Scrum Master and identify some strategies to build that trusting environment.

Commit to actions and add them to the next sprint backlog:

The team may suggest some improvement ideas. As an example, they may suggest trying out a new digital tool which has come out on the market to find out if they can use the tool for automated testing. If it works, they can stop doing manual testing which takes a few days of the sprint. So, it is an experiment. It was not in the product backlog and not a product feature either so the Product Owner may think it is not important. Improvements include what is necessary for the process of developing the product, therefore the Product Owner should support and prioritize this technical experimentation.

HOWEVER, IF WE are talking about larger scale products, in terms of several features, geographical expansion or customer demographics, then we need to think about how to scale up the product development. That is where we have to talk about different Agile product set-ups for scaling products. We will discuss different approaches in the next section.

Scaling product development using Agile

In most production environments, there is a strong focus on the development stream at team level. As a consequence, the small development team will be fully functional and productive using Agile cadence, process, and practices. However, other supportive functions also will be needed to operate at the same speed. There is multiple other parallel work required to make the product commercially available. As an example, when the product is ready with a few of the most important features, it should be able to launch to the customers. Hence, the work required to launch the product to the market and provide the business support should also be ready, along with the product features. Let's examine what is required to make the product commercially available.

Product commercialization

Introducing a new product to the market is a whole different ball game. As an example, Apple might be in the process of developing its next iPhone. Features they want to include may be already in the research and development phase. Some features might have been completed. But Apple has not launched the product yet to the external market as product is not yet ready as a full product. When the product is launched to the general public, the iPhone (let's say 14) should be able to be manufactured on a massive scale. So, the manufacturing plants need to have enough raw materials to manufacture the new model. They also should upgrade their machinery and working capital (manpower) in order to do this.

Then the partners, such as telecom service providers like AT&T, T-Mobile, Etisalat (UAE), Singtel (Singapore), Telstra (Australia) should be ready to market the new iPhone. They should update pricing strategies on their websites, make promotional sites available to market the new phone etc. So, there are many other requirements to scale a product in the commercial environment.

Just because the product is developed does not mean it is ready to sell to the customers at the scale the company expects.

Let me give you another example from the real estate sector. In the property market, sometimes marketing and sales campaigns start even before the construction of the house or housing schemes begin. Construction of the property and the sales and marketing happen simultaneously. As a result, when the construction finishes, some customers are ready to sign the lease immediately or buy the property and move in even before the smell of the paint evaporates. I was such a customer.

All started with a letter in my post box four years ago. The letter explained that a new property development would start in just two months and the property would be completed in eighteen months. Along with the letter I had a nice information pamphlet showing pictures of one, two and three-bedroom apartments and inviting me to an exclusive event showcasing a display unit they had built at the site. The following weekend I visited the display unit which was an exact replica of the two-bedroom unit they were building. When I ask where the building would be, they showed me empty land just opposite the display unit. Apart from a few machines moving around and digging soil there were no buildings. But I could see the work had started. And at the end of the month, I put down a deposit for an apartment that did not yet have foundations.

During the waiting period, the sales team kept me updated on the progress of the development and a countdown to completion. Sometimes they invited me to the construction site, which was a mess. They did the construction in iterations. That means that once the foundation and structure of the entire building were done, the rest of the interiors were developed in iterations. Since my apartment was on the third floor, I was part of the first iteration. Once the construction was finished, I was one of the very first people to move into the building. As a result of marketing & sales working parallel with construction, their time to market the apartments was minimal. Whole units were sold out even before the foundation was laid. And when the development was completed, almost all apartments were occupied immediately. Sales and marketing did not wait to complete the construction to sell the property.

Products should be able to launch as soon as development is finished. Hence, other functions required to launch the product need to work parallel to the product development.

As we have seen that applying Agile as a process and a new way of working for the development team has been successful, it also should be adopted by the other functions required for the success of the product. These functions also can be structured and follow a similar cadence parallel to the development structure and cadence.

How the parallel functions/teams should be structured using Agile

As the owner of the product, you should focus on all the aspects of the product not just the development of the technical solution. It is your responsibility to make sure the product is ready to launch.

A product launch can be feature by feature or combined features or on-demand as requested by the customers. This strategy is defined as the product roadmap. That means other functions should work parallel to make the product ready as per the product roadmap strategy and timelines. Let's classify these different functions into three categories as 'enabler stream/team', 'development stream/team' and 'launch stream/team'. These streams can be structured as illustrated below.

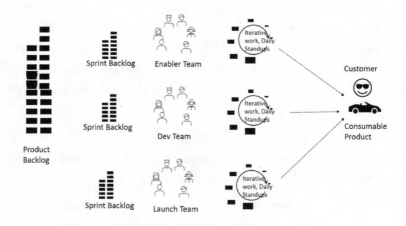

Figure 15: Integrating enabler, development and launch using Agile

Enabler stream/team

Let's assume you are the owner of a corporate banking application which helps loan approval. There is a legacy system which needs to be retired and you have been identified as the Product Owner for the new product development.

Enablers required for this new software product may include modifying the enterprise architecture to remove the legacy system and to integrate the new system. Probably it may include moving to the cloud so that the new product is future proof, as well as procurement required to hire necessary resources etc. So those functions will be part of the enabler stream.

These streams also can be structured using the same small Agile team concept and following the Agile cadence of two weeks like the development team. They also should follow sprint planning, daily standups, sprint showcases and retrospectives. They also should synch with the development and the launch streams to support the final goal of launching the product on time to the customer.

Figure 16: Sample composition of an e-Commerce enabler team

Development stream/team

We discussed the development stream in detail in the previous chapter. This stream is the nucleus and the core of the product development. The Enabler stream should be ahead of the development team in terms of timelines and the launch and process/advisory teams need to run parallel to the development team.

Launch stream/team

This stream/team should facilitate the launch of the product external to the mainstream product development. That can include planning tradeshows with partners, channel partners, sales and marketing, after-sales service teams etc. As an example, once the loan approval system is developed it needs to be marketed and sold. There may be a partner who is using the legacy product and now these partners should be prepared to use the new product.

Functions like call center also should be integrated as when a customer calls and ask for help the call center should be in a position to answer them. So, it should be structured using the same Agile practices.

Figure 17: Sample e-Commerce launch team composition

Product structure for larger products

Some products are larger and complex. Such products need multiple development teams, probably multiple Product Owners, and multiple support teams. However, if we can apply the Agile values, principles, practices to all teams and all levels, then we can still deliver the value faster to the customer by minimizing waste. That is where Agile at scale comes into the picture.

As we have seen, we can apply Agile at team level using frameworks such as Scrum, but there are also other frameworks which support larger products. One such extremely successful framework is the Scaled Agile Framework (SAFe). SAFe enables the alignment of 125 to 150 team members. That is nearly ten teams.

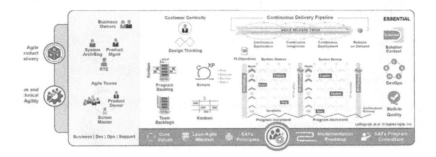

Figure   18:   SAFe   team   structure   and   process
(safeagileframework.com,2020

In this framework, all teams are aligned in the same cadence. Each team picks user stories from the Program/Product backlog and adds them to team backlogs. All product features developed by each team are continuously integrated into the main product and at regular intervals (i.e., at the end of the sprints), each team showcases the developed versions to a bigger audience. At the end of several sprints, nearly eight to ten weeks, they release the product to the market if that is still applicable as per the product launch strategy.

The SAFe framework has been a big success, but specific knowledge is needed to apply the framework to larger solutions. I would recommend Product Owners producing complex products get help from a SAFe program coach or consultant.

Summary

Often enough, for enterprise level product development, which may need several million dollars of strategic investment, it is necessary for multiple teams to work in parallel. To get the best results from Agile, all these teams needs to be structured and operate using the Agile principles we discussed previously. Just one team working in Agile will not be able to deliver enterprise level products to the market. Hence, the Product Owner's understanding of how to structure such enterprise level product development in the Agile way is paramount to success.

References

ScaledAgileFramework, 2020, Essential SAFe, Retrieved from safeagileframework.com

CHAPTER 4
THE PRODUCT OWNER ROLE

The Product Owner has a critical role in product development. This visionary and servant leadership role has been defined uniquely by every Agile framework. Below is some literary research on how this role has been defined.

As we discussed previously, the Scrum Agile framework is special as it is a widely used and popular small-scale Agile framework. The Scrum framework explains the Product Owner role as below.

Scrum alliance definition of Product Owner

> The Product Owner defines the what; as in what the product will look like and what features it should contain. The Product Owner is expected to incorporate stakeholder feedback to create the highest value product increments each and every sprint. Product Owners maintain the product backlog and ensure that everyone knows the priorities.

According to the Scrum framework, the following are the responsibilities of a Product Owner.

- Clearly express product backlog items.

- Order the items in the product backlog to best achieve goals and missions.

- Optimize the value of the work the development team performs.

- Ensure that the product backlog is visible, transparent, and clear to all, and shows what the Scrum Team will work on next.
- Ensure the development team understands items in the Product Backlog to the level needed.

The Scrum framework also mentions the attributes a Product Owner should have as the following.

- Empowered. Has decision-making authority for the product.
- Business-savvy. Knows the business, the customer, and the market.
- Persuasive. Able to work well with the team and the stakeholders.
- Knowledgeable. Knows the market and the product. Grasps production challenges.
- Available: Is readily accessible to the team and to the stakeholders.

(ScrumAlliance.org, 2020)

A similar definition is provided by the Scrum.Org, another professional body which is a leader in the Agile environment.

Scrum. Org definition of Product Owner

> The Product Owner is responsible for maximizing the value of the product resulting from the work of the Development Team. How this is done may vary widely across organizations, Scrum Teams, and individuals. The Product Owner is the sole person responsible for managing the Product Backlog.

They further explain the responsibilities of the Product

Owner as the following.

- Clearly expressing Product Backlog items.

- Ordering the items in the Product Backlog to best achieve goals and missions.

- Optimizing the value of the work the Development Team performs.

- Ensuring that the Product Backlog is visible, transparent, and clear to all, and shows what the Scrum Team will work on next; and

- Ensuring the Development Team understands items in the Product Backlog to the level needed.

One important point to highlight is about the authority of the Product Owner. The Product Owner should have the authority to decide and make decisions on the product. According to Sutherland J., Schwaber K (2020) 'for the Product Owner to succeed, the entire organization must respect his or her decisions. The Product Owner's decisions are visible in the content and ordering of the Product Backlog. No one can force the Development Team to work from a different set of requirements.'

Large Scale Scrum (LeSS) definition of the Product Owner

Another important Agile framework which helps large scale product/solution development is the Large-Scale Scrum (LeSS). It defines this role as follows.

'Product Owner is responsible for maximizing product value, prioritizing *items* in the *Product Backlog*, and adaptively deciding the goal of each Sprint based on constant feedback and learning.'

Scaled Agile Framework (SAFe) definition of the Product Owner

SAFe helps to apply agile at the enterprise level. If properly applied it can transform larger corporations using Agile values, principles, and practices. Even if it focuses on enterprise-level transformation, it relies on team-based product development. Hence SAFe defines the Product Owner role as follows.

'The Product Owner(PO) is a member of the Agile Team responsible for defining stories and prioritizing the team backlog to streamline the execution of program priorities while maintaining the conceptual and technical integrity of the features or components for the team.

The PO has a significant role in maximizing the value produced by the team and ensuring stories meet the user's needs and comply with the definition of done.'

Also, some interesting research has been conducted about the Product Owner role. According to Hrafnhildur Sif Sverrisdottir et al. (2014), 'The PO role is one of the most important roles in Scrum and often the most difficult one. He is responsible for the financing of the project during its life-cycle and he puts forwards the requirements and objectives of the project'. The researchers further say 'the most important task of the Product Owner is to make a decision on what should not be prioritized and take the consequences of that decision. It is imperative that he rejects new requirements that are not necessary, in collaboration with the stakeholders and the team, instead of adding new unnecessary requirements to the PB.'

What is very clear from these definitions by different agile bodies and from research is the significance of the Product Owner role. All frameworks recognize the same set of responsibilities of the Product Owner. In the next section, we will examine these responsibilities in detail.

Responsibilities of a Product Owner - a Deep Dive

Put simply, the Product Owner's job is to develop a product. This product is part of the strategy of the company. Hence developing a product is strategic work. There are many decisions to make such as how the product can meets its expected benefits; how to gain market share; improve the productivity; reduce the waste or increase the customer satisfaction. If strategic goals are missed it could even push the company out of business. Hence the product you are going to develop is paramount to the growth of your business so the Product Owner's job entails a lot of responsibility. Let's look at this responsibility in depth.

Understand the problem which the product needs to fix

Let's assume the Product Owner has to build a house for a customer. Before doing anything else, the first thing the Product Owner should do is understand why the customer needs a house. Without understanding this, you may build a house identical to the one customer is living in right now. There would be no added value for the customer if that happens. In fact, it would just be a waste. The product you build should meet many of the customer's needs. Customer may be able to explain the needs/requirements or not. But as a Product Owner, you must be visionary in order to understand, not only the current requirements but even the future requirements in order to add value to customer.

As an example, say your customers are a recently married couple, planning to have three kids. The new house should be able to cater for three kids in the future. It should have a backyard where kids can play. Probably a swimming pool so the family can have an outdoor experience during the summer. Perhaps a game room for kids. A newlywed couple may not even imagine these features, but the Product Owner should be able to envision these future requirements to truly add value to the customer.

As you can see, it is vital for the Product Owner to understand what the customer needs because the Product Owner represents the customer or the user. There are multiple techniques, methods and tools to explore problems which need to be fixed by products. These will be discussed in later chapters in detail.

Understand the stakeholder needs

The product is not going to be built in isolation. As an example, let's take the house we discussed above. It is not going to be constructed just by the Product Owner. There are various parties who need to get involved in such a development. This will include the team: an architect, builders, electricians, plumbers, masons, which we can call the development team. In addition, there will be the city council for construction approval, utility companies for water, electricity and telephone connections, cleaning service providers and banks for financial approvals.

These parties have various requirements, all completely different from each other. Hence when we talk about maximizing the value to the customer, we should also talk about these parties, as unless we partner with them, the product may not be able to deliver maximum value within the specific timeframe. Hence it is important to understand stakeholders and their requirements and working arrangements as well.

Understanding the stakeholders is one thing and understanding their requirements is another. Bringing them to one table is an entirely different thing altogether. It's easy to listen to and cater for requirements in isolation. But some requirements overlap. Compromise will be necessary as the product will be developed within constraints. As an example, let's say users who are going to live in the house want to have minimum electricity and water bills when they start living there. This requirement conflicts with utility service providers who want customers to have ways to maximize utility consumption as that is how they earn money. To provide maximum value to the customer, it is necessary to have a constructive discussion between both parties to find a mutual way to benefit each party.

The Product Owner needs to understand different stakeholders and harmonize everyone's vision to develop the product. How to do this will be discussed in a later chapter.

Understand internal and external constraints

The Product Owner will deal with many constraints in the process of building the product. Sometimes these constraints are visible and sometimes they are not. Knowing these constraints will help the Product Owner to be prepared for the worst and will help to increase the value to the customer.

As an example, there are some costs when building a house. For the construction, there is the cost of labor and materials. Then there are service, utility and connection costs. The longer the duration of the construction and building, the heavier the costs. What if the work has to be redone due to a mistake? Then the costs will increase. But what if the authorized spending is just one million? The Product Owner should know the limitation he/she has in terms of expenses. And let's say the customer needs the house in six months. This is a time constraint. Another external constraint could be, for example, if there are very old trees in front of the land and the city council has enforced the preservation of these trees. In this case, no trees could be cut during the construction process or there would be a breach of the law.

These constraints, internal or external, define the limits the Product Owner must work within during the construction process. He/she must therefore be aware of the limitations and constraints before and during the building process.

Understand the processes and tools

What process needs to be followed when building a house? What materials should be used? Concrete or other materials? Is it sustainable to use wood for the window work or would aluminum fit? What is the process in order to get city council approval? Does the construction need approval? These are the questions relevant to the process of building a house.

The same applies in the IT or business-related product development process. Since we are focusing on Agile, what is the Agile process? Has it been used before? What are the terminologies? What is a 'sprint'? What is a user story? Who is a Scrum Master? What is cadence? The Product Owner must know the answers to these questions.

When I look at the difference between a great Product Owner and an average Product Owner, what is always noticeable is how much great Product Owner(PO)s know about Agile as a methodology. More than understanding the Agile methodology, they have the 'Agility' mindset. They are open to ideas, empower the team, trust the Agile process, respect the team, users and the process. That definitely makes the product successful and eventually those Product Owners successful as well.

Build the team

The Product Owner may not have all the skills required to build the product. Therefore, it is necessary to identify these skills and recruit the people with the right skills. The team will materialize the Product Owner's vision.

Once the team is identified and recruited, the Product Owner needs to understand the team very well and build a healthy professional relationship with them. The Product Owner should be aware of many details about his/her team members: their background, what they studied, even if possible what their family background is, what skills they have, what skills they need to learn, their career aspirations, what they like to talk about and what they don't like to talk about. These details are very fundamental and very essential to build a good rapport and relationship with the team.

Understand the limitations of the authority

The Product Owner role is a leadership role. That means the Product Owner has to make decisions in the process of building the product. We can say that the Product Owner has a certain authority. However, does the Product Owner have full authority to do anything he/she decides? The answer is that the Product Owner does not have full authority unless he/she is spending his/her own money.

This is not only from a monetary perspective. Even from a time perspective or sometimes in terms of product features, Product Owners may not have full authority. So what kind of authority does the Product Owner(PO) have? What can he/she authorize and what can't he/she authorize?

As an example, in a commercial environment, if the product is e-commerce software, the Product Owner may not have the authority to select the development framework of Hybris or Magento. It may need to be authorized by the CTO of the organization based on the IT strategy. So, it is important for the Product Owner to understand what authority level he/she has and who are the other people he/she should refer to when such decision-making is required.

Understand the competitive products

This is more applicable in the commercial environment where the products you build have counter products in the market. Why would the customer buy your product? What competitive advantages does your product provide over other products? If the Product Owner creates the same products as the competitors, he/she will not be providing value to the customer and as a result, the company may not be able to get a competitive advantage. But if the Product Owner starts a complimentary product, the Product Owner can even partner with the competitors to create maximum value.

This is nicely explained by Mark Randolph, the founder of Netflix. When he was trying to figure out the Netflix business model, he did not try to replicate Blockbuster which was already selling DVDs. Instead he searched for gaps in the market and found that no one was offering DVD rentals. So, he started a DVD rental business where the DVDs were delivered to the doorstep. Since he did not try to replicate other business models, he did not have to worry about competitors. In fact, there were no competitors for the product he was offering (Mark Randolph, 2019).

In this process, a good product owner must have many skills to do the job. In the next section, we will examine these skills in detail.

Skills a Product Owner should have

When a customer loves a product, they will make it part of their daily life. And if they really love it, they very rarely move to other products.

Here is an example from my dear friend Wissam. For Wissam, owning the latest iPhone is part of his social status. The day the new iPhone model is released, he instantly transforms himself from 'Wissam' to 'Wissam who owns the latest iPhone'. Kind of like a celebrity. He is constantly in touch with Apple and he pre-orders the iPhone just before the new release. When the order arrives, he is probably one of the very few people in the office to have the latest iPhone. Then everyone in our office gets to see the new iPhone through Wissam and to our surprise, he is kind of a Guru who knows all the iPhone features. His explanations tempt us to buy one. We do not need to go to the IT helpdesk to get help with our iPhone issues. We just give Wissam a call and he tells us 'do this and that' and the issue will be solved. He advises us how to use the iPhone to improve productivity, what apps we should download etc. Even people working in Apple cannot argue with him when he explains something about the iPhone. He is crazy about it. I've known him for more than ten years, and he would not use a Samsung phone even if it were given to him for free. A few of us purchased Apple products just because of him.

But when it comes to a customer like me, it is quite different. I do not care about the brand of the product. What I need is durability, quality and a product within a reasonable price range. My needs are very specific. As an example, there are these small earbuds which I have fallen in love with.

For a long period, I was searching for good wireless earphones. Being on wireless is important for me. I travel. I jump from this meeting to that meeting. Sometimes I have to dial in to meetings while I am on the train or in transit. So, it is quite difficult when two wires are hanging from my ears and around my neck. I desperately wanted wireless earbuds. I tested the different products from Bose and Sony, which were extremely expensive. Then I found some other wireless earbuds of the same quality, but not from a big name like Bose or Sony. I gave them a try. And I fell in love with them. They fit my ears. They do not fall from my ear when I jog. One charge of the battery is enough for ten hours of meeting time. And they are super cheap. So, I purchased two sets of them. Not only that, I promote them to all my friends who have the same need. I've been using this product for more than two years now and I have not even listened to any of the promotions from Sony or Bose. I never wanted to because I am happy with this cheap product even though it does not have a big brand name or a celebrity status.

Do you see the difference? Two customers (Wissam and myself), have two different requirements. But when we love a product we don't even look at competitor products.

That is why building products that customers love is particularly important. And as a Product Owner, unless you develop products liked by your customers, your product will not be successful. However, developing such a product is not an easy job. You must find a balance between managing costs and increasing the quality of the product. So let's see what skills you need to build such products.

Obsession with customer experience

It should be the customer's role to explain requirements. The problem is customers cannot always do this. That is the idea behind the famous Henry Ford quote, 'If I had asked people what they wanted, they would have said faster horses'.

Fifteen years ago, I worked as an IT business analyst for an aviation company. We had to develop a new software product which would enable them to plan their entire annual revenue and to manage it throughout the year. My job was to sit with the customers and understand their requirements and then explain these to the software development team who was accountable for developing the software product in line with customer requirements. Getting the requirements from these highly educated customers, who were senior leadership level people, was very difficult. They could explain what they were doing at that moment, but they were not able to explain what they wanted in the future. Some of them were doing that revenue planning daily, but when I asked them to explain how they were doing it, they could not explain it, even though they knew how to do it. So if we developed the software based on what the customers explained, we would have ended up developing a set of Excel sheets because that was how they were planning.

To understand the customer requirements beyond what they can explain requires a special mindset. Customer experience is much more than understanding customer requirements. It is necessary to think from a broader perspective. That is, human-centric design. The Product Owner needs to think about the profile of the customer. Based on that profile, how can we create the best customer experience? To do that we need to think about things like: what is the customer's age group? what is the customer's background, his/her family, his/her job profile? what does he/she need to make him/her successful? It is necessary to delve into what he/she thinks, what he/she says, what he/she feels etc. From customer to customer this profile is different. Even if it is the same product, depending on the customer profile, the experience of the product is different.

Trying to understand customer experience is a new skillset. If the product does not deliver a good experience for the customer, it will be useless and valueless to the customer. Hence one of the important skillsets a Product Owner should develop is to obsess over the customer experience. Wearing the hat of the customer is a mindset change. Adopting this mindset is critical for developing customer-centric products.

Active listening

Everybody listens, but active listening is 'listening with a purpose'. That purpose is to learn. The Product Owner needs a lot of information from many people, customers, stakeholders, the team etc. All of them hold information the Product Owner does not have. Obtaining that information from them is a skillset. One way to get this information is 'to listen to learn'.

As an example, the customer has the information regarding what he/she needs from the product. The team knows a lot of things such as technical feasibility. Suppliers/vendors know a lot of competitor information and the market trends etc. So, if the Product Owner develops the skillset to listen to learn then he/she can get a lot of information otherwise not available.

My experience with Product Owners is that they are more talkers than listeners. Most of the time, Product Owners are senior managers in the organization. They have the authority that comes with the hierarchy. If they maintain the same authority and try to overpower then they may not be able to listen to the 'untold' stories or information given by customers, stakeholders, or the team. It requires a hell of a lot of effort to stop the urge to talk instead of listening.

In the process of developing the best product for the customer, collective knowledge is essential. To obtain that knowledge, the Product Owner needs to be an active listener. A listener who listens to learn.

Clear communication

The Product Owner interacts with many stakeholders, customers, team members, project/program managers, Scrum Masters, subject matter experts, end-users, partners, suppliers etc. The number of people a Product Owner must interact with can be very overwhelming. As an example, the Product Owner of the previously discussed e-Commerce solution had to interact with the following parties.

- Sales and Marketing managers who will be used to sell their products.
- End users who will buy products using the e-Commerce site.
- The development team, i.e. architect, software engineers, software testers, content creators, IT support personnel etc.
- The Scrum Master who are part of the development team.
- Agile coaches who is part of the development team.
- Account partners and technical team of the payment gateway company such as PayPal, Visa, MasterCard etc.
- Delivery partners such as the national postal service provider, Uber, DHL or FedEx or any other delivery service providers.
- Packaging service providers.
- Marketing and branding service providers.

These people are from different companies and have their own businesses and interests. Their educational background, the language they use, the interest they have in this product are quite different from one person to another. As an example, an Uber driver may not even understand the service level agreements (SLAs) while the SLA is very important for the delivery timelines of the product.

Regardless of their background, expertise, educational level, career level, they are essential partners of the product development process. The Product Owner needs a lot of information from them and they need a lot of information from the Product Owner as well.

Hence how the Product Owner communicates with these partners is an essential component in the success of the product development process. How the Product Owner communicates with an Uber driver may be completely different from the communication with a DHL delivery partner. Yet all these parties must be engaged in the right manner in the product development process. Thus, communication is key.

How to be better at communication

Communication is a very broad and complex subject. Even politicians, scientists and top-level executives in organizations struggle with communication. What is clear to one person may not be clear to someone else. Hence communication is always a tricky business. The Product Owner can focus on the following points to be effective in communication.

- Be clear about what you want to communicate

  Spend some time in understanding the message you want to communicate. Do you want to communicate a decision you made, or do you want some information from the stakeholders? What is the purpose of your communication? You may need to spend some time understanding what exactly you want as the outcome of the communication, because depending on the outcome you need, your communication medium should change.

* Select the best communication medium

Is it a press conference? Is it a town hall kind of mass gathering? Is it a newsletter? Is it a news bulletin? Is it a one-on-one closed-door communication or is it a brown bag session? Depending on the outcome you are hoping for, the communication medium should be different.

If you want to get approval and get a contract signed, the best communication medium may be a face-to-face, one-on-one meeting. But if you want to communicate a decision made, such as the product road map, then a town hall kind of mass media, a brown bag session or an email would be ideal. If you want to get feedback on a product feature you have developed, then a product trade show combined with a survey or interviews will be ideal. So, to get the maximum benefit you need to use the best optimal mode of communication.

As an example, you may have seen how Apple introduces a new iPhone model. They do that via an annual keynote session which they organize once every year. But they don't do the same when they are discussing a manufacturing contract with a manufacturing plant in China. And for the iOS updates every quarter, they don't host such keynote meetings. They simply send an email saying the iOS needs to be upgraded.

As a Product Owner, you need to have a very good understanding of these communication mediums. If not, you will not get the expected benefit. As an example, if you do a Standup via WhatsApp chat, you may not be able the get the right update from your team. So, it needs to be a co-located, face-to-face group gathering.

- Analyze the audience/recipients

Who are you addressing? What is it that they need from you in order to give you what you need from them? Do they understand the language, words, jargon you use? Do you need a translator?

As a Product Owner, it is essential you understand the audience. Especially when you are working with technical people such as software engineers or scientists. Also, we are living in a world where production lines are more and more global. Some of the product team members may be in countries where the language you use is not their mother tongue. So, if you use some slang they may not understand. Your focus here is how to get the best value from them by integrating them into the production process. That can be done only if you understand your audience well.

- Plan your communication

Having a town hall kind of mass communication at lunch hours needs a lot of preparation. You need to arrange lunch otherwise your audience is not going to join you. If you plan it at 4.30 p.m. you are not going to get them onboard either. That is the time they want to catch their train or pick up the children from daycare. So your town hall will be the lowest priority of your audience. Having a standup meeting at 8.30 in the morning is not going to be a very positive experience either.

So you need to plan your communication.

You may need to write down your message, rehearse

it if it is a speech. Plan the venue, meeting rooms, video setups and finally the logistics, food etc. These will be different from communication to communication.

- Confirm understanding

  Let's say the Product Owner informs the team about the prioritized product features. It is an important decision because your team is going to focus on the priorities and invest time and effort to implement these. What if they misunderstood your priorities? Then they will implement wrong product priorities. Hence clarify if they have understood what you communicated before they move into action mode. It will help to reduce a hell of a lot of rework and waste.

  There are many ways to clarify if the recipient has understood what you communicated.

- Summarize what you just talked about.
- Ask your team to summarize for you or to explain their understanding.
- Record it and make it available for their reference if possible.
- Send the decisions made and agreed on as a written email.
- Be available to clarify any doubts.

Decision-making

One of the very critical skillsets a Product Owner needs to have is 'decision-making'. Product development involves so many decisions throughout its journey. Those decisions will include strategic and operational decisions.

What product features to implement and what product features not to implement, along with the best time to stop development and kill the product, are some of the critical decisions made by the Product Owner. These decisions will decide the life of the product and the value the product is going to deliver.

The downside of this decision-making is that if an incorrect decision is made, this could result in waste and delay the value delivery to the customer. It will reduce the return on investment of the product and the business may suffer from the wrong decisions.

Decision-making can be stressful as many people are dependent on those decisions. But if the decisions are the right ones, then it can produce high return on investment and a happy customer, which results in a profitable business.

The Product Owner needs to be very comfortable with decision-making. Some decisions need to be made on the spot with a limited amount of data. Sometimes there will not be any data at all but the decisions have to be made. So how to make the decision and how to use the available data to make the decision is extremely difficult for someone who is not comfortable with uncertainties. Let's say the Product Owner has developed the e-Commerce site and now has to decide on how to charge the customer once he/she orders the products. Let's say the payment gateways like PayPal or Visa charge 3% as the transaction fee which will increase the product price. But if it is 'cash on delivery' then there is no transaction fee. But then there is a risk that the customer will not pay. So, it is a decision-making point whether to go ahead with the payment gateway with no risk but an increased product price or to go with cash on delivery with a risk of non-payment. It is a stressful process, but it is critical to the success of the product.

Collaboration

As the Product Owner, you need inputs from many people to develop the product: customers, partners, suppliers and end-users, to name a few.

Hence it is essential that the Product Owner finds a way to collaborate with all these partners. The collaboration will be more successful when all of them can work as one team. All input has to be taken constructively.

Co-location has great merit for collaboration. When everybody is in one place sharing the same space, it allows them to break the ice and get familiar with each other. We have seen that co-located teams produce the products at a much faster speed. That is because co-location increases collaboration and reduces communications gaps. It just takes a moment to go to a whiteboard and start ideation on how to solve something. Even when there are different companies as partners or suppliers, if they can co-locate, they start working together towards one goal.

However, some organizations or people, do hesitate to co-locate. One reason is the conflict of interest. But as the Product Owner, this is where you have to use your authority. You know co-location is the best option so you must make it mandatory for them to co-locate. You can include terms in the contract to make co-location a contractual obligation.

Domain knowledge

Let's say as the Product Owner your job is to build a ship. What kind of knowledge do you have about ships? Sailing? Or at least water-based transportation? This is domain knowledge. When you are the Product Owner who must create a product, your subject matter expertise is essential for various reasons.

When we talk about the business systems and the products required to assist the business, the amount of information the Product Owner knows about that industry is extremely helpful to develop the product. He/she is not expected to be a master in that business, but at least a good knowledge of the business is required.

Let us take the example of an e-Commerce product. What is e-Commerce? Why is e-Commerce required? Which business does this e-commerce product relate to? What products are going to be sold using e-Commerce and can those products be sold on an e-Commerce site? Are these chemical products? Can you sell chemicals online? What regulations apply when selling these products? What does the manufacturing process look like? This is the domain-related information which is essential in the process of developing the e-Commerce product.

Why is domain knowledge essential? The Product Owner must make certain decisions on behalf of the customer. Also, the Product Owner needs to collaborate with people who are already in the business. For example, when the supplier is talking about 'bill of materials' or 'HS codes', the Product Owner should at least have some understanding of what the supplier is talking about.

It may not be possible to acquire the same knowledge as the people who are already in the industry, but at least the Product Owner must reach a very good understanding of how the business is operating. Therefore, if the product you have to build is not from your industry, you must spend a good deal of time learning everything about that business and sector. It will make the product development process easier.

Servant leadership

As a Product Owner, you are a leader. You must work with a lot of other people to develop a product to deliver to the customer.

There are many ways to get things done. You can use the authority given by your place in the hierarchy to get things done using the command and control way or in other words 'bossing around' or you can empower the teams and collaborate. The impact of the leadership style in a product development environment cannot be underestimated.

In our research, what we have seen is that those who use servant leadership develop better products. The job of a servant leader is to 'serve others' such as customers, partners, suppliers, the team, and the end-users. His/her job is to work for them. Not the other way around. Agile is built upon servant leadership so has been very successful in the product development process. In the Agile method, everyone is a leader. The job of the Scrum Master and Product Owner is to serve others. They set aside hierarchies and don't even bother about their title or the authority given. This is a big mindset shift for a lot of people.

I once had a Product Owner who owned a banking product. Working in a traditional bank he had a command and control mindset. He told others what to do and others did what they were told. But once we started using the Agile method, we coached the Product Owner to change this mindset. He understood and was in the process of moving towards 'servant leadership'. However, after some time, old habits came back. After a few sprints, the product development team became tired and were kind of feeling the pressure. I observed what was happening by sitting with the team. I realized that the Product Owner, who was very busy with a lot of other things, wanted the work to be reviewed daily. Instead of coming to the standup in the morning, he asked the team to stay back. No matter the time, the team had to wait until he came to the team for reviews. Sometimes it was 5.30 p.m. and the Product Owner conducted reviews till around 7 p.m. Sometimes the team went home after 8.00 p.m. because the Product Owner came to them only around 6.30 p.m. In addition, the following day, the team came back to the office at 9.00 a.m. sharp to do standups. I knew this process was killing the team's productivity because their body language said everything. They were tense and looked exhausted. They just did the work because they had to.

So, during the team retrospective, we asked the team what needed to change and what was not working. Initially, the team did not say anything because they did not want to draw attention to themselves. But when we reassured them that it was a safe environment and the intention was to make things right for them, then one by one they admitted that working late hours and waiting for reviews done by the PO was killing them. More than anything they felt it was not fair. They nicely worded it as 'if the Product Owner can plan the reviews earlier then we can finish and go home on time'.

We then discussed this feedback with the Product Owner.

We explained that if the team continued like that, the Product Owner was not going to get the best output from them and they may even leave the company. The Product Owner had not realized that his style was impacting negatively on the team. He was not used to the process of getting feedback from the team. But that insight was an eye-opener for him, and he appreciated it. So, the next day he apologized to the team and asked for the team's suggestions on how to make it right. They suggested having the reviews immediately after the standups in the morning and that would help them to do the adjustments required and finish the day on time. The Product Owner agreed, and organized everything around the team's needs. He prioritized the team, making himself available for them. That product became one of the very best products in that bank and the team was recognized as one of the bank's best teams as well.

Thus, adopting a servant leadership mindset can be very hard but it is one of the essential qualities a Product Owner must cultivate.

Self-organization

You may have realized by now that, as a Product Owner, your job is everywhere. There are many people to meet, there are many things to learn and there are many things to do. That means a Product Owner is a busy person. The Product Owner may feel that 24 hours is not enough time to get things done. That is also the reason it can lead to stressful situations and why Product Owners may adopt a command and control leadership style. The Product Owner's self-organization is key.

A big workload should not mean that the Product Owner spends 18 hours a day in the office. He/she should not have to miss out on family life. It is essential to have a healthy work/life balance. Hence organizing the day, week, month, and prioritizing so he/she, focuses only on the value-added activities, is an essential skillset for a good Product Owner.

How to self-organize

In the process of organizing your work and life, consider the following.

- Take stock of everything you need to do (this is your backlog)

  Create a list of things that you need to do, people you need to meet, events you must attend etc. If you have a dedicated desk in your office, then write down all these on post-it notes and paste them under a column named 'My Backlog'.

- Prioritize the list by shuffling based on the value it adds to your team, product and to you personally.

  Then categorize these into a small bucket of what must be done today, next day etc. That will allow you to plan the week.

- Allocate some time every day or week to do this exercise. As an example, I block my Monday morning every week for this. I do not accept any meetings from 9-11 on Monday morning as that is my weekly planning time. I prioritize the things I have to do, classify the things into days, plan other meetings I need to have within the week and send the meeting invitations. If I have to send a status update report, I block time in my calendar for that. This way, all the people I am working with get meeting invitations in advance. And that also helps me to prepare for my meetings. If I have to prepare a solution proposal on Thursday, I know that on Monday, so I have enough time to prepare and get the details.

- And lastly, time box it. Agile highlights the concept of time boxing. When you know you have only one hour for product prioritization, then you will focus on getting it done in one hour. Respect the time. When you know you have one hour and not more than that you will not derail for less value-adding tasks or distracting conversation.

- Getting self-organized requires discipline and changing habits, but when you get organized it is extremely powerful and essential to the success of the job you must do.

In the process of acquiring these skills, it is worthwhile to check the options a product owner has in the formal or informal education.

Product Owner's educational background

How does one become a Product Owner? Not just an average Product Owner, but an exceptionally good one. A Product Owner who delivers value to the customer, the business and the team.

It is a reasonable question, especially because when you are in college or university, you may not be taught to be a Product Owner, whereas for certain career paths, there are very specific instructions and courses etc. As an example, if one wants to become a doctor you go to medical school. If you want to become a lawyer, you go to law school. And if you want to enter the corporate world, you go to business school. But there are certain careers paths that are not so clear, and product management is such a path. So let's try to figure out what educational background can be followed to become a product manager/owner.

Everyone is a product manager/owner

Anyone can be a Product Owner or manager. If you can develop a product from scratch and if you can commercialize it and if it adds value to someone, then you can be a Product Owner.

As an example, some time ago, I discovered that I was good with photography. Not only did I like to take photos, I liked creating artworks from photos and some people admired my work.

Sometimes people asked me to do photo shoots of them and they offered to pay for it. I thought I could do something with this, and I decided to create some photo books from my travel photography and sell them online. It all started with that thought. There were some customers, and I had the resources, so I started creating artworks and selling them online by creating an e-Commerce site and constantly producing artworks. Throughout this process, I had to work with multiple suppliers like website builders, payment gateway processors etc. But I was the one who decided what I wanted to build, what I wanted to sell, when I wanted to sell, and when I should shut down the product etc. I converted raw materials into a product which added some value for some customers, and I made some profit from the sales. So, I was the Product Owner of my own business.

You, also, may have done something similar on a small scale. But when there is a commercial purpose, when we develop products with the purpose of delivering a service to customers and expect monetary returns, then there are things we should learn beyond the small scale.

The formal path to becoming a great Product Owner is supported by a combination of factors like experience, formal education, professional education, and deep passion for such work.

Learning by doing

Have you heard of Thomas Suarez? He was just twelve years old when he stood on the stage of TEDx. In his first TEDx speech, he talked about his journey in mobile app development. He explained how he got into mobile app development and the kind of apps he developed over a period of time.

When you listen to that journey, you realize how mature he was in that app development process. Most people fall into the trap of just developing apps. But he was different. Even though he started it as a fun project while studying in junior school, he had done a lot of research which made his app successful. He named his first mobile app 'Bustin Jieber'. Commenting on the app, he said that a lot of kids in his school did not like 'Justin Bieber', so he created this app as a game by mocking the name (how to attract customers). His app was simple yet attractive enough to make the user (his fellow friends in school) addicted to the product. The App had a picture of 'Bustin Jieber' and he moved across the screen. The game was to catch him, but it was hard as Bustin moved fast to another location before the gamer could get him. But if he did get caught, the app gave a reward.

Figure 19: Screenshot of Bustin Jieber app

What makes him so brilliant for a twelve year old teenager was his business-minded thinking. He launched this app just before the school holidays. (planning based on external events to create product road map). During the holidays, parents normally do not put any restrictions on how long kids spend on their phones. So, he planned well. Also, it worked very well because kids had something new to do during the holidays (value to the customer). Not only that, kids had something to talk about or brag about when they came back to school. 'Hey, I caught Bustin. How much did you get? I earned 240...'(kids showing off).

At the age of twelve, what he did was the job of a Product Owner. He carefully planned how to add value to the customer, create a market segment, research it, plan the road map and then develop and release the product. He then measured the success and stopped the product at the right time.

Becoming a Product Owner is a hard job. It is rewarding but it can be stressful. You need to know a whole lot of things to keep going. It is not like getting an idea and dropping it halfway when confronted by difficulties. Resiliency is necessary during the development process and you need to learn from experience until the results are achieved.

In a commercial environment, nobody would develop products for fun. As explained in the previous chapters, products help to realize the strategy of the company. So being a Product Owner is a serious job.

No business will allow anyone to be a Product Owner just because you have a passion for this. You have to demonstrate enough experience in the commercial/business environment. Hence experience in the business environment comes into the picture when one wants to become a Product Owner.

When I look back at some extremely good Product Owners I have come across, they were not freshers in the job. They had nearly seven to ten years' experience in business although in different domains. They were in a position to 'lead', make an argument, and had the courage to say 'NO' when required. They had the experience of collecting information to make informed decisions and they had the experience to meet a C-level executive and explain why a product feature needed funding to develop it.

So, you need enough experience and knowledge to be a very good Product Owner. If you are planning to be a good Product Owner, first focus on getting the relevant work experience of developing something. You can shadow a good Product Owner in your work and get some coaching and mentoring.

Formal education

This is a tricky one. Mark Zuckerburg who developed Facebook did not graduate from a university. But it didn't matter because even before university he had already started developing the software he wanted to build. So, he already knew the product life cycle. He learnt it by himself by doing the job.

He started learning software engineering when he was fourteen. So, he had the technical knowledge required to develop the product. From fourteen years to his first year in university he was programming which gave him enough time to master it. So, he did not obtain a formal degree, but that did not stop him from developing one of the best products in the world because of years of experience.

In commercial environments, we have seen that successful Product Owners do have college degrees in various disciplines. One of the exceptionally good Product Owners I met had a BSc in Architecture and an MBA and he was developing products for a real estate company. His formal education in architecture and the business knowledge gained from the MBA helped him to know the technical side and the commercial side of the products he was developing.

Another very good Product Owner I know has a marketing degree. After ten years of doing different jobs, she moved into product management in the marketing space. Her formal education in marketing helped her gain theoretical knowledge of the audience she was working with. And the same helped her to think about the product features the customers would expect from the marketing software which she was responsible for developing.

There are many examples I could give to conclude that formal education would greatly benefit product development in various subject areas. It is beneficial to have education in a specialized discipline. Education, combined with some experience in the business environment, is extremely helpful to be successful in the job.

Professional Certifications

If the Product Owner is serious about becoming a great Product Owner, there are a few skills to acquire and luckily there are some good courses which teach those skills. Since this book has been focusing on product management in an Agile way, I will list a few courses which will help you to learn the methodology.

Agile product management

There are various Agile Product Owner training courses. These different courses are based on the Agile frameworks. Fundamentally, all agile frameworks follow the Agile manifesto, values and principles. In that sense, everything will be the same. However, different frameworks do have their own unique practices integrated into the frameworks as well. Read on to understand the differences between each of these frameworks and to get some guidance on which course and certification you should acquire.

Certified Scrum Product Owner-CSPO

Figure 20: CSPO badge (scrumalliance.org, 2020)

Certified Scrum Product Owner is a curriculum offered by Scrum Alliance. Scrum Alliance is one of the oldest and largest Agile foundations. It is a members-driven, non-profit certifying body in the Agile space (scrumalliance.org, 2020). Since its establishment in 2001, it has trained more than one million Agile professionals in the world and I would assume it is the only foundation which can claim that many professionals trained as at 2020.

CSPO is based on the Scrum framework. This is the

basic training anyone can start. You will get to learn the Scrum framework, its fundamentals, Scrum practices etc. Finally, it will introduce you to the Product Owner specific training.

During the two days of in-house training, you will learn about the role of the Product Owner in the Scrum team, his/ her responsibilities etc. Then you will move on to the concept of user stories, how to write user stories, techniques on splitting user stories and maintaining the product backlog etc. You will also have some hands-on experience with groups in the class which will definitely help.

At the end of the two days, you are expected to sit for an online test to validate your knowledge. Upon passing the exam you will be able to claim the certification and the badge. If you are new to Agile and product management then this curriculum can establish a good base.

Advanced Certified Scrum Product Owner- A-CSPO

Figure 21: A-CSPO badge (scrumalliance.org, 2020)

When the Product Owner has basic knowledge and some experience as a Scrum Product Owner(PO), the Advanced Product Owner(PO) curriculum can help you to expand your knowledge in advanced topics. With this course you will be able to learn concepts like product vision, multiple product integrations to form multiple business initiatives and working with multiple stakeholders or multiple teams. Please refer to the web page of the Advanced certified Scrum Master of Scrum Alliance for further details and to find a course:

https://www.scrumalliance.org/get-certified/product-owner-track/advanced-certified-scrum-product-owner

Scaled Agile Framework (SAFe) track

SAFe is a framework which I admire. Especially because it creates a particularly good foundation to scale Agile at large enterprise level. When we develop solutions for an organization with several thousand people in multiple countries, we need a way to apply Agile at the enterprise level. And it can be very difficult. Scaled Agile Framework has been making good progress in this space.

Large organizations generally have large solutions programs. The e-Commerce product example in this book was in a large organization which had nearly 80,000 people. That product involved more than one team across multiple countries. Such products are developed by multiple teams and depending on the scale and the time, may even involve ten to fifteen teams with nearly ten or eleven members in each team. The SAFe framework was established to use Agile practices at a larger scale. This course teaches this framework and Product Ownership using the framework.

SAFe Product Owner/Product Manager

Figure 22: SAFe Product Owner/Product Manager badge
(www.scaledagile.com, 2020)

- This specific course will teach the attendee the following:
- How the Scaled Agile Framework is structured and terminologies
- SAFe values, principles, and practices
- How these values are applied to the Product Owner role
- Concepts of Epics/Enablers/Capabilities/Features and breaking down these to user stories
- Product backlog creation concepts and prioritization techniques
- What is the Product Owner's role and responsibilities towards the agile team and the Program Increment (PI) planning.

This two-day course is pretty hands-on. It will have a nice balance of theoretical knowledge and practical knowledge through carefully designed exercises. At the end of the training, the attendee is expected to sit for an exam within thirty days and pass the test with a score of at least 77% to get the certification.

In my experience conducting this training, most of the attendees obtain very good knowledge from this course. Especially those who come from larger organizations. However, I also found some people did not get any value out of it because they did not have any sort of Agile experience or experience in larger organizations. So they were not able to understand some concepts we teach in this class. Hence, I would suggest first you get some experience working in an Agile team before you try out this course.

You can reach this information by vising the web page https://www.scaledagile.com/certification/certified-safe-product-owner-product-manager/#examdetails.

Other Agile certifications

Apart from the above frameworks, there are multiple other Agile Frameworks like Large Scale Scrum (LeSS), and Nexus by Scrum.Org.

Large Scale Scrum (LeSS) offers product development on a larger scale. It combines multiple scrum teams to form a synchronized larger solution or product. LeSS is structured in a way that each team is responsible for developing a product feature. As an example, let's say the e-Commerce website is developed by one team and the e-Commerce mobile app is developed by another team.

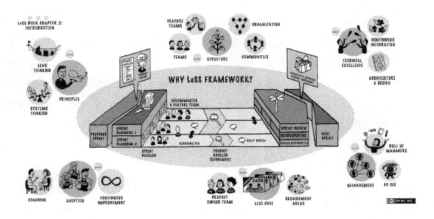

Figure 23: LeSS framework structure (LeSS.works, 2020)

Each team needs to be synchronized to develop the final product. To develop such a large product, multiple Product Owners are required to deliver on the agreed cadence as depicted by the figure below.

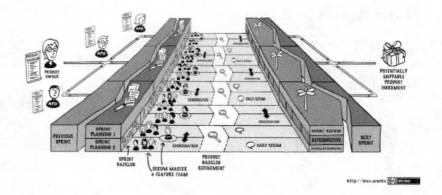

Figure 24: Multiple Product Owners synchronized together to deliver multiple product features (LeSS.works, 2020)

LeSS introduces the concept of Product Owner and Area Product Owner (APO). The APO manages the feature team backlog while the Product Owner manages the entire product backlog. There are also various courses in this framework. The Product Owner can find the details on this page: https://less.works/courses/less-practitioner.html

Nexus by Scrum.Org

Nexus is also a scaled scrum framework offered by the organization Scrum.org. This framework also has gained popularity in enterprises especially where they are required to develop larger products.

Scrum.Org provides three levels of Product Owner certifications: Professional Scrum Product Owner 1; Professional Scrum Product Owner 2 and Professional Scrum Product Owner 3. Depth of knowledge and level of complexity increases with each level. You can view the details of this course by accessing the Scrum.Org website: https://www.scrum.org/professional-scrum-product-owner-i-certification

NEXUS™ FRAMEWORK

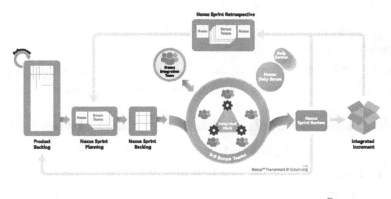

Scrum.org

Figure 25: Nexus Agile Framework structure (Scrum. org,2020)

Stacking certification versus gaining knowledge

Having a deep knowledge of product management is very advantageous. It will help the product, stakeholders, customers, and the business. Hence getting deeper knowledge and acquiring skills are necessary. However, this should not be confused with stacking certifications.

Certifications do not equate to knowledge or experience. One may have all the Product Owner certifications without the hands-on experience of implementing a user story. Some people gravitate towards acquiring certification after certification but without any knowledge. Knowledge is how the Product Owner applies the things they learnt in real-world situations. The Product Owner may be able to apply the knowledge as it is. Or else the Product Owner may use that knowledge to invent something new in the practical world. Proper knowledge is required for that. Because real-world products or stakeholders are not going to react or respond to the exact way these certifications teach you. These frameworks courses will offer the basic knowledge and based on that you will be able to apply that to the real-world situation.

The number of certifications that the Product Owner has is irrelevant if he/she does not know how to maintain the 'flow' or sustainable limit of work the team can do. Hence focus on getting the knowledge rather than a pile of framework certifications.

Who should be selected as the Product Owner?

Who should be selected as the Product Owner? When it is decided that a series of products are necessary to realize the business strategy, the first question is, who should lead the product development? However, we need to think about developing products using Agile methodologies from various angles, rather than just finding someone to lead the product development. Hence who should be selected as Product Owner is a tricky but important question.

It is possible things can go wrong when selecting the right Product Owner. Most of the time, existing roles are remapped into Product Owner roles. Research conducted by Milos Jovanovic et al., 2017, revealed a similar finding from five different teams who were responsible for software products. Below is the old and new role mapping in those five teams.

Team	Old role	New role
T1	Systems Architect	Product Owner
T1	Software Developer	Scrum Master
T2	Systems Architect	Product Owner
T2	Systems Architect	Scrum Master
T3	Project Manager	Product Owner
T3	Software Developer	Scrum Master
T4	Project Manager	Product Owner

T4	Requirements Engineer	Scrum Master
T5	Project Manager	Product Owner
T5	Requirements Engineer	Scrum Master

Table 5: Research findings on role mapping (Milos Jovanovic et al., 2017)

Although the research does not give more details about the product, this mapping is simply shocking. In the above teams, some project managers or systems architects were assigned to the Product Owner role. Chances are these products were technical software products and if they had the right skills and knowledge to be a 'Product Owner' is doubtful. Especially in the cases where a project manager was assigned as the Product Owner.

Another pitfall I have seen is assigning IT Business analysts to the Product Owner role. Shockingly most of these business analysts come from external consultancy companies who have no experience in the client company they were hired for. Even more shocking is to see that they are being hired as contractors for six months or twelve months. Some product development is lengthier and can take years to complete its lifetime. Hence six month or twelve month contract assignments are very misleading and unsustainable. Also, the Product Owner needs good domain knowledge and a lot of leadership skills. People who come from external consultancies do not have the same knowledge as the people in the client company so such assignments are not sustainable.

Thus, selection of the Product Owner is serious business and should be thought through very strategically. Below are some guidelines to select the Product Owner.

Select the Product Owner from internal staff

If our intention is to develop the best product which

addresses customers' needs, the best we can do is to recruit the Product Owner from internal staff. Internal staff have the business and domain knowledge, they know the internal and external stakeholders and they know the internal processes and tools. As we discussed in the previous chapters, these are all essential to develop a product. Using internal staff will enable a faster delivery of products to the market as the learning curve for internal staff is minimal compared to that of an external consultant.

The concern most leaders have about assigning an internal employee to the role is that they may not know the Agile process. That is where an Agile coach comes into the picture. When we move into the Agile process, the Agile coach will suggest the path. He/she will suggest the training and certification for the Product Owner. During the development, the Agile coach will coach and mentor the Product Owner in the process. Hence an Agile coach can fill the gap in Agile knowledge.

Select the Product Owner with domain knowledge

I explained the importance of having domain knowledge. Depending on the target system or the product, select the Product Owner accordingly. As an example, if the product is a marketing product, like marketing software or a series of digital channels, select the Product Owner from the marketing community. There are multiple advantages in selecting the Product Owner from the same domain. One advantage is the ease of getting the change management required to introduce the new product to the company.

Along with the product development, change management is the hardest part. As an example, if the product is a Customer Relationship Management system, then once the product is developed it needs to be introduced to the customers who are the sales and marketing community. When the Product Owner is from the community of sales or marketing, it benefits product development because he/she understands the needs from the sales and marketing perspective. The Product Owner is the voice of the customer and it is easy for him/her to represent the customer. When it comes to the change management part, the sales and marketing community are more likely to listen to someone from their community than someone from a different domain like IT or an external consultant.

Select someone with authority and servant leadership

We previously discussed the Product Owner's involvement in decision-making. Hence the Product Owner should be someone who can make the right decisions at the right times. Hence it may not be good to select someone who is very junior. For example, an intern who is doing their first job may not be suitable to be selected as the Product Owner because he/she may lack the authority. However, it is subjective and should be on a case-by-case basis as sometimes even the most junior person may have better leadership skills than a more senior person in the organization. It depends on the person and the type of product.

As an example, let's say the CEO says that he/she needs to prioritize the implementation of a particular product feature over a feature that has been prioritized by the Product Owner. How would the Product Owner react to such a demand coming from the person with the highest authority? When the candidate is junior, they will be intimidated by the hierarchy and implement the CEO's priority immediately. But a good Product Owner with leadership and the right authority will try to understand the CEO's request on this occasion and would then get the data and facts to demonstrate that implementing the CEO's product feature is not the best option. Saying 'no' needs some courage and authority at the right time. A Product Owner with the right leadership will not be scared to have a challenging conversation without getting intimidated by the hierarchy.

Product Owner's career path

If you've been a Product Owner for a few years, you might be thinking, what next? Some people feel bored with the job after some time. Of course, for some it is not a question at all, as long as they work on different types of products, or because they feel comfortable with what they do and the products they are developing. But some people want to know what their next step is.

Maslow's hierarchy of needs

Career progression is a psychological need. Especially in large corporations where thousands of people work.

After some time, most people expect to move up the ladder. This allows them to take on more responsibilities and earn respect in the corporate environment. An accountant could become Chief Financial Officer over a period. What is the highest level a Product Owner can achieve over a period of time?

Figure 26: Maslow's hierarchy of needs (Maslow, A. H. (1943)

Based on what I have seen and experienced in many organizations, the answer to this question is not clear (probably not many people have really thought about it). This may be due to the fact that Agile is still new in many organizations. Companies start projects in Agile but how the organization is structured to support these projects is still not figured out. As a result, the career path for Product Owners, along with Scrum Masters, and Agile coaches is a grey area.

Below is some guidance on this area. However, how things are done and how things are structured is completely up to the organization.

Product Owner

The role of Product Owner is the entry point for an Agile career path. The candidate might come from a business analysis background. If the person has a good understanding and in-depth knowledge of the domain and industry, along with some knowledge on how Agile works at the team level, they can become a Product Owner. We have discussed the necessary knowledge, experience and qualities in detail in the previous chapters.

In most cases the Product Owner will take care of only one product if it is a small one, for example an e-commerce website. They will work in only one team and be accountable for one product backlog. In some Agile frameworks, they may have the title 'Area Product Owner (APO)'. This is the same as 'Product Owner (PO)'.

Product manager or Chief Product Owner

In some organizations, Product Owner and product manager are two different roles, with two different positions in the hierarchy and two different functions. In these cases, the Product Owner is at the team level whereas the product manager is one level above in the hierarchy. Thus, the Product Owner reports to the product manager. However, both titles can refer to the same role.

Some organizations which have moved to an Agile organizational structure, do not have the designation 'product manager'. Personally, I believe we should get rid of 'manager' titles. Especially if your organization is embracing Agile and building the future roadmap with Agile values, principles and practices. A more appropriate role definition would be 'Chief Product Owner'.

A Product Owner can own a small product like a mobile app to be delivered within three to six months. That mobile app may be just a feature of an Epic like Digital Omnichannel across the organization. Other teams will be developing the e-Commerce website and the retail shop. The product manager (or the chief Product Owner) owns the entire product as a larger product backlog. The Product Owners own subsets of that big product backlog.

The difference between the two roles is the scope. The Product Owner's scope is somewhat narrow compared to the product manager/Chief Product Owner whose role encompasses product vision and the roadmap.

It is essential to have many years experience as a Product Owner to take up a higher role such as product manager/ Chief Product Owner. Product feature synchronization to make the working product, rather than just fragments, is a huge responsibility because individual items may work in isolation but when integrated it may not work. Strategic thinking, exceptional leadership, excellent negotiation, and organizational skills are key to being successful in this role.

Product Director or VP of products or Product Portfolio Director

Different organizations give this role different names. Regardless of which title is used, this is the next level of the hierarchy. Products may be categorized by theme or geography. As an example, if it is CRM, it is possible to have a Product Director for CRM. So, the director of the products will decide what features to be included and in what regions it should be implemented and drive the strategy using the CRM.

Chief Product Officer (CPO)

Some organizations, especially startups or pure product-based companies, have come up with this senior role. This role is at an extremely high level in the hierarchy often at the same level as C-suite. The Chief Product Officer (CPO) will take care of a series of products rather than just one product. It is a strategic leadership role.

Often this role defines the direction of the organization. The CPO collaborates with the Chief Executive Officer (CEO) who sets the strategy of the company, the Chief Operating Officer (COO), Chief Technology Officer (CTO), Chief Marketing Officer (CMO) and any other C-suite role, such as the Chief Data Officer (CDO) and Chief Information Officer (CIO). The organizational strategy and goals are defined by these roles.

The CPO will report to the board or CEO. The person in this role will be responsible for return on investment directly and for the growth of the organization. The CPO will most likely define market strategies, for example how to enter the Middle East and African markets. He/she will also determine which new product lines should be introduced and why.

The entire organization may be heavily dependent on the product portfolio managed by the CPO. Decisions made by the CPO could have an impact on whether the company exists or not. Take, for example, Apple. The iPhone, iPod, MacBook and iPad are the bread and butter of the organization. Apple thrives due to these products. How well the product is manufactured and designed, and how well the product attracts customers, determines if Apple can thrive as a company. This role works with a strong research arm. A CPO needs to be a visionary. To think a few decades ahead.

When you are mapping your career path, you should focus on the scope and growth of the area you would love to work in.

Title should matter least. There is no point having a title like 'Chief Product Officer' if you don't know how to set up the go-to-market strategy. However, you do need to take career development into your own hands, as not many organizations care about this.

References

Maslow, A. H. (1943). A theory of human motivation. Psychological Review, 50(4), 370–396. https://doi.org/10.1037/h0054346

Craig Larman & Bas Vodde, 2014, The LeSS Company B.V., retrieved from less.works

Scrumalliance, about us, 2001, retrieved from scrumalliance.com

Scrumalliance, 2020, Advanced Certified Scrum Product Owner(PO), retrieved from scrumalliance.com

Scrum.org, 2020, Professional Scrum Product Owner(PO)1, retrieved from scrum.org

SclaedAgile.com, 2020, SAFe Product Owner(PO)/Manager, retrieved from ScaledAgile.com

TEDxManhattanBeach, 2011, Thomas Suarez, A 12 year old app developer, retrieved from ted.com

Mark Randolph, 2019, That will never work - The birth of Netflix and the amazing life of an idea, Octopus publishing, London

Sutherland J., Schwaber K, 2020, Scrumguide, Retrieved from Scrumguide.org

Hrafnhildur Sif Sverrisdottir, Helgi Thor Ingason, Haukur Ingi Jonasson, The Role of the Product Owner in Scrum-comparison between Theory and Practices, Procedia - Social and Behavioral Sciences, Volume 119,2014

Product Owner,2020,retrieved from https://less.works/less/framework/product-owner

Product Owner, Scaled Agile, Inc, 2020, retrieved from https://
www.scaledagile.com

CHAPTER 5
THE PRODUCT LIFE CYCLE

Any product goes through different phases during its lifetime. Depending on the type of product it may have multiple, high level phases. It can be summarized as below.

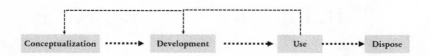

Figure 27: Product life cycle

Conceptualization

The product is conceived at the helicopter or macro level. High-level information such as a business case, strategic theme or an epic statement can be found at the strategic leadership layer. The C-suite leaders know that an initiative needs to be taken or an issue needs to be addressed but until it reaches the conceptualization stage, nobody knows the details of how this will be done. Not even whether it is an IT solution or a business solution etc. At the conceptual level it is necessary to form a concept of the product. What is the exact problem which needs to be addressed? How it is connected to the strategy? What are the benefits expected at strategic level? What happens if it cannot be addressed? What sort of products are needed? What is the budget? What are the constraints, for example, time constraints? What is the exact product? Lots of details need to be determined, with the collaboration of many people.

At this level, a product canvas and a concept of the minimal viable product (MVP) will be created, along with a product backlog with high-level product features. A product roadmap will also be created. We will find details about these in upcoming chapters.

Development

When you reach the development phase you have received all the necessary approvals for the business case or product canvas you provided at the conceptual stage. You have the green light to start the development. At this level, you develop features of the MVP. In other words, the team will start to be fully functioning and materialize the product concept.

This is the phase where the product is in the development team's hands. The Product Owner will identify the product features and its return on investment. Based on that, features will be prioritized and the development can begin. The full product will be developed iteration by iteration. Each product feature developed will be tested with real customers and its usability checked.

This phase will involve the Product Owner working with all the enablement teams, launch teams and development teams, along with stakeholders, end-users, suppliers, vendors and partners. The developed features will then be combined and released to the customer to use.

Use

This is the phase where the product is released from the production house into the hands of consumers. Customers started using the product and when they find value, they will start paying. They are able to measure the benefits or the value they are getting from the product. For example, if the product is a digital banking mobile app, customers will see the value in terms of time saving and faster loan approval etc.

During this phase, consumers will provide feedback. They

may be impressed with the product and feel it is worth the money they paid. Alternatively, they may be disappointed. In that case, they may complain about the product and write negative feedback. They will call you and say it is crap and they might even demand their money back. Customer feedback is the real testimony for the success of the product.

Sometimes while using the product, customers may encounter some issues and they will call to get these fixed. If the issues repeat, then it could be a bug or a defect in the product. This will need to be fixed in future products. You may remember that some time back Toyota recalled all their Corolla models as they had detected a failure in the breaks (Product Safety Australia, 2020/18295).

They did a global recall to get all the cars out in use back into the manufacturing plant in order to fix the issue. In the IT world sometimes the IT system might need to be temporarily stopped until the issue is fixed.

The use phase is when you start to see the benefits of the product. It will start to generate income when it is purchased by the customer. Or if it is a product to improve productivity, customers or the business should be able to see this improvement. As an example, if it is an online loan approval system, you should be able to measure the impact of the product by looking at the number of loans approved within a week and comparing this with the figures before the product was introduced. Say the lending department processed only 2,000 loan applications a month before your product was introduced, but after they started using the product, 6,000 loans were approved within the first month. This means your product has helped to improve productivity threefold.

Leaders will want to be able to measure the impact so they know if the strategy is working.

Dispose

This is the phase where the product comes to the end of its life. This can happen for various reasons such as poor customer satisfaction or outdated technology, or less return on investment as the cost of production is higher than the returns. The Product Owner has to make the decision to stop production and prepare to end the product completely. Now the team will be moved to other products as the same production capacity is not required. You may also move on to develop a new product, leaving behind the product you worked on for a long time.

In the next section we will discuss product conceptualization in detail.

Product conceptualization and Strategy

Why do you have to develop this product? Why is it so important to your organization? What benefits are expected from the product once it is developed and released to the market? What would happen if the product were not developed? These are the questions we need to be clear about before we begin and invest time and effort developing any product.

How does it all begin? A ten-thousand-foot view

Products don't start just like that. There is a rationale behind every product. Products are the bloodstream of every business and there is a story behind each one. Some products are the result of a light bulb moment. Some are carefully planned around the business and others are developed to solve a problem. Think about the examples below of how products started their journey.

Uber

Uber's revolutionary business model dates back to 2008 when its co-founders Travis Kalanick and Garrett Camp attended the LeWeb tech conference in Paris. As the story goes, both were waiting outside the conference hall, shivering in the winter cold and desperately trying to get a taxi back to their hotels. They tried to hail taxis, but none stopped because it was peak hour and all were carrying passengers. Out of frustration, while trying to figure out why the taxis weren't stopping for them, they had a light bulb moment: 'What if we could book a taxi in advance via a mobile app?' That was the beginning of Uber (Travis Kalanick, 2012).

Initially started as 'UberCab', it went through a journey to become the Uber of today. As we speak now, Uber has become part of our daily life. It has gone beyond its original product conception and expanded to provide other services such as delivery. The value of Uber became even more evident during the COVID-19 pandemic as it offered delivery services for those stuck at home. This is exactly the way a product can solve a problem.

Now some products emerge in very strange ways. And some begin as just fun projects and later become products. Some products originally do not solve any sort of problems, but later become part of big solution providers. One of the best examples of this is Facebook.

Facebook

Mark Zuckerberg, as a fresher in Harvard, developed 'Facemash', a website which allowed Harvard students to compare two female student pictures and vote for the more attractive. This 'social website' became an overnight sensation and crashed the Harvard servers when everyone started using it. It started as a fun project for Mark, which he did from his Harvard dorm room. But that unexpected popularity made him think about a bigger picture. He tapped into the very complex subject of 'social connection'. He later expanded this concept of social connection to the outside world, making Facebook a phenomenon in the last two decades.

Although it started as dorm room entertainment, Facebook

became a very integral part of human society. We have heard of families reuniting via Facebook. Adopted children finding their biological mothers via Facebook. Humanitarian initiatives via Facebook etc.

Solving problems

There are hundreds of similar stories behind every product. Read about Netflix, Airbnb, Amazon and you will find that all these products tried to solve a big problem. The problems might be wide, global problems. Or they might be simple and applicable only to the enterprise or business division you are working in. However, it is really important to understand what the problem is we have to solve through the product.

Products that do not solve a problem or add value will not be embraced by users and will fail to generate any revenue for the company. That is why the Product Owner should always ask the questions 'Why do we have to develop this product? What problem should it solve? What returns are expected?'

Product development is a long, labor-intensive process. Some products will take years to get to consumable level. Roadblocks may appear which will force you to give up or shut down the product. There will be derailments. Managers will change, CEOs who fund the product or COOs could change. However, when the product vision (that is, why we develop the product) is clear, it allows the product development journey to continue regardless of what changes occur. It is a gravitating point when there are derailments. Hence, it is important that the Product Owner either develops the product vision or if it has been already developed, that he/she understands this in detail.

In the commercial environment, products are always connected to the strategy. These strategies might have been classified into multiple themes, as explained below.

Strategic themes

In commercial environments, the idea of developing a new commercial product originates from various discussions, analysis, and future planning. These discussions take place in boardrooms where all the leaders in the organization discuss how to reduce costs or increase profits or how to provide a solution to a social problem existing in society.

Most of the time these strategic level discussions happen at the beginning of the financial year. People like the CEO, COO, directors, and business leaders get together and examine the previous year's financial records. They will see where they have had strong growth and where they have not. This process itself is long and subject to debates, agreements, disagreements etc. Most of the times they will do something called SWOT analysis at this level.

SWOT analysis

Leaders will look at their business' strengths and weaknesses when developing the strategy. These will be either measured in a tangible way, for example financial performance or intangible ways like brand awareness, international presence, or the company's strong partnerships. Then they will look at what opportunities they have in the next financial year. As an example, if the company is in the transportation business and a country where they operate wins the next Olympics, then it is an opportunity for the company to try to win a contract for visitor transportation during the Olympics.

They also think about what threats they face in the next financial year. As an example, if the company is a TV channel, Netflix is a threat because viewers are moving to Netflix rather than watching their channel. This will reduce their consumer base significantly so they must do something.

As an example, below is a SWOT analysis for a restaurant;

S

Good reputation among customers
Good customer review in Yelp
Good location in CBD
120 corporate partnerships
Reputed head chefs
High sign-up numbers
Location is ideal
Affordable prices

O

Develop a vegan recipe
Olympics coming to the city in four years' time
Celebrity catering
There is a culinary school nearby in the city
   (could hire staff   from them)
Expansion of corporate catering and events catering
Renting out the restaurant for corporate events

A single location means minimum growth
Number of customers did not grow last
year
Staff retention has become an issue
Cost of ingredients has increased
Rent has increased

There is a vegan restaurant opening next door
The young generation is health-conscious and
   searching for vegan food
Organic ingredients are extremely expensive

W   # T

All these areas will give a strategic focal point to the senior leadership. Even the threats can be converted to opportunities. The threat of expensive organic ingredients can lead to the idea to purchase homegrown products or, better still, grow the products at the restaurant itself. These identified focus areas will then be converted to strategic themes which the leadership can develop in the next financial year.

Strategic theme template

Strategic themes can be explained in various ways. Some formats are very lengthy, and some are samples and serve the purpose. Since we are focusing on Agile, a method which identifies ways to deliver more value by eliminating waste (such as excessive documentation), I would like to introduce the lean strategic theme template proposed by the Scaled Agile Framework.

The Scaled Agile Framework provides a very good way of explaining strategic themes. It is called Objective and Key Results or OKR. This method provides a way to explain the strategic theme and key results expected once it has materialized. Below is an example of OKR for the 'Grow our organic food' strategic theme.

Objective	Key Results
Grow our organic ingredients	Increase the customer base by 10% (organic food lovers)
	Reduce the cost of the ingredients by 15%
	Increase customer satisfaction ranking by 25%

Figure 28: Strategic theme template proposed by Scaled Agile Framework (Scaled Agile,2020)

Strategic themes to products

Strategic themes are the senior leader's interpretation of how they should tackle the issues they identified at the leadership level. This is the strategy to win more customers or gain more market share or expand the business. Each strategic theme needs to be implemented to get results and the results should be measurable as in the above template.

When it comes to implementation, these strategic themes will further be divided into multiple initiatives for the sake of focusing on each implementation. This is where we talk about epics and enablers.

Enablers and epics

Epics and enablers are the major initiatives which originate from the strategic themes. Scaled Agile Framework describes an epic as follows:

'An Epic is a container for a significant Solution development initiative that captures the more substantial investments that occur within a portfolio. Due to their considerable scope and impact, epics require the definition of a Minimum Viable Product (MVP) and approval by Lean Portfolio Management (LPM) before implementation'. (Scaled Agile Framework, 2020)

An enabler is explained as follows:

'An Enabler supports the activities needed to extend the Architectural Runway to provide future business functionality. These include exploration, architecture, infrastructure, and compliance. Enablers are captured in the various backlogs and occur throughout the Framework'. (Scaled Agile Framework, 2020)

Epic and enabler are both significantly larger breakdowns of strategic themes and will be implemented to realize the strategy. If we take the example of the 'grow our own organic food' strategic theme, 'organic vegetable garden' will be an epic while 'irrigation system' will be an enabler. Both of these need to go hand in hand for the 'grow our own food' strategy to materialize.

Epics

Epics are larger items. An epic can take years to implement. It will need multiple teams and millions of dollars of investment. Nobody invests such a large amount of time and money for nothing. Think about how long it takes to prepare soil, add fertilizer, find the perfect plant, plant it, water it every day, all this because you are expecting one fine day it will bear some fruit. When implementing an epic, a huge return is expected, as explained in the strategic theme template. Implementing epics is a monetary business.

Hence before implementing an epic, a cost-benefits analysis is needed. If you are a senior product manager or a chief Product Owner, then you will be involved at this level. The following is a format which can be used to identify the epic details.

Epic Name	
Epic Description	FOR [Customer] WHO [needs something/do something] THE [Solution name] IS A [How] That [value] Unlike [Competitor] Our Solution [does something better – Why]
Business Outcome	Measurable benefits the business can anticipate if implemented

An example epic for an e-Commerce solution would be:

Epic Name	e-Commence iOS app
Epic Description	FOR Millennials WHO need to order items on the go THE e-Commerce Mobile App IS A Mobile solution That enables access to stores on the go and delivers the items within 24 hours Unlike ZPrice app Our Solution delivers products in 24 hours
Business Outcome	250,000 USD monthly revenue via mobile app (Based on 5,000 new mobile users making 50-dollar orders monthly)

Each of these epics/enablers can be a single product or multiple products. If you are a Chief Product Owner at the senior leadership level, then you will be involved at this level. Otherwise, you will be just an owner of one of the products. Regardless of which level you are at, it is always an advantage to know how the product you develop is connected to the strategy. This is the macro or ten-thousand-foot view of the product you are going to develop.

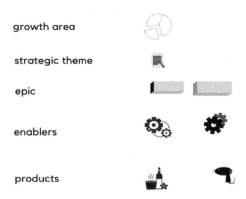

growth area

strategic theme

epic

enablers

products

Figure 29: How products connect to the strategy

As a Product Owner you will be provided with the epic level description or the strategic theme level description. The leaders will then hire you to develop the product they identified. However, if you have not been provided with the above information, before you proceed you should immediately clarify using the templates above. The reasons are clear. You are going to be held accountable for implementing a product with strategic investment and it should deliver benefits to the company. You should fill out the above details and get validation from the senior leaders before you move forward. It will help to avoid confusion in the middle of product development.

References

Scaled Agile Framework, Strategic Themes template, 202, Retrieved from https://www.scaledagileframework.com/strategic-themes/

Travis Kalanick, (2012), youtube.com, Retrieved from https://www.youtube.com/watch?v=rQ6GoY2_Ujw

Product Safety Australia, 2020/18295, Toyota Motor Corporation — Toyota Corolla Hatch Hybrid (ZWE211) and Corolla Hatch Petrol (MZEA12) MY2020, Retrieved from https://www.productsafety.gov.au/recall/toyota-motor-corporation-toyota-corolla-hatch-hybrid-zwe211-and-corolla-hatch-petrol-mzea12-my2020

CHAPTER 6
DESIGN THINKING & PRODUCT DESIGN

At the early stage of the product life cycle or at the conceptual stage, we want more details about the product. As you have seen, it starts at the strategic theme level. You might have been provided with the strategic theme, epic statement or enabler statement. Perhaps all of them or nothing at all. Whatever your situation, you need to start from the little details provided to you.

When you come in at this level, all you have is a series of questions. How can we increase sales? How can we increase market share?, How can we increase staff productivity? How can we do this and how can we do that? All these are questions which have been given as a strategic theme or epics or enablers. Hence as the Product Owner, your job is to go beyond that level and find sustainable answers. Your job is to find solutions via the product which you are about to develop.

In the quest to find answers to all these questions, you can use a very powerful methodology which has proven to be very effective. This methodology is not something new. It has been used for a few decades but in the last decade it became very popular and gained much recognition. It is 'Design thinking'.

Design thinking or Human-centered design (HCD)

When we talk about developing products that customers love, our main focus is the customer (as a reminder, the customer is the consumer, employee, partner or suppliers). Likewise, when we talk about delivering value to the customer, our main focus is the customer. The customer needs to be the central, focus point and we need to organize everything around the customer to address everything he/she needs. That is where 'Human-centered design (HCD)' comes into the picture.

HCD gained attention in the past decade as more and more companies started using it. However, the original story of HCD goes back to 1978 when one of its pioneers, David Kelly, started his design company 'David Kelly Design'. Later, Kelly co-founded IDEO which is considered a forerunner in applying a human-centered approach to innovate and solve problems (IDEO.com,2020). IDEO helped to design the very first mouse called 'Lisa' for Apple computers. As you have seen that product has grown to be a product which all of us love. It is very simple, sleek and serves its purpose and function. Nothing more, nothing less.

Figure 30: Mouse designed by IDEO for the Lisa computer: The Apple computer (IDEO.com, 2020)

According to IDEO, Human-centered design is an interactive approach which uses an iterative process called 'design thinking'. Design thinking contains empathy-driven discovery, rapid creation, reflective evaluation to ensure outcomes are driven by the unique preferences and circumstances of the people they serve (IDEO, 2015). The process of applying human-centered design into problem-solving (how might we) has been hugely successful and it has now been used in hospitals, the aviation industry and many other industries.

HCD as a process puts the customer at the center and a solution emerges from there. This approach has helped to develop revolutionary products across various industries. The solution or possible solutions emerge as an idea first. Then those ideas are validated again and again through prototypes and rigorous customer testing until they are developed as feasible and viable solutions. It is a constant learning, unlearning and an iterative process.

With every iteration, there are tests to see if the solution is working or not. If it does not work, why? The solution becomes closer to what the user needs. According to IDEO, this process helps to find a solution desired by humans, viable for business and feasible to implement. Hence the success of this methodology is phenomenal in almost every application.

I was lucky enough to learn this methodology while working at IBM Interactive Experience (IBM Studio) some time back. We helped our clients to apply this methodology to crack huge strategic business problems faced by clients in various industries like banking, aviation, telecoms, retail, healthcare etc. And I do not recall a single instance when it failed. All our clients were able to develop groundbreaking business solutions and products using this methodology.

HCD uses a methodology called 'Double Diamond'. As a Product Owner who needs to develop a product which customers love, this methodology could be useful for you. So, let's look at it in more detail.

Double diamond

Double diamond has, as the name suggests, two diamonds: Diamond 1 and Diamond 2. In the first stage or the first diamond, we try to understand the problem exactly. So let's call the first diamond, 'Problem Diamond'. In the second stage or Diamond 2, we try to identify the solution. Let's call it 'Solution Diamond'. Within each diamond there are two phases. First, we diverge and look out. Then we converge and narrow down.

That means in the first diamond or the Problem Diamond, first we diverge and see different problem statements and then we narrow down (converge) and finalize the problem. In the second diamond or the 'Solution Diamond', first we expand and see possible solutions and then we narrow down and nail down the final solution. At each of these phases, we use multiple tools and generate various artifacts as explained in the next section.

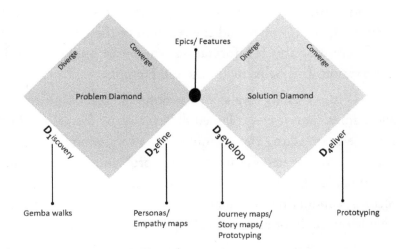

Figure 31: Double diamond

D1 - Discover the problem

In this phase, we try to understand the problem. Is there even a problem at all? If so, what is the real problem? For example, why aren't our customers happy with our products? Why have we lost market share? Why do we get so many complaints from customers? How can we bring back our customers? These questions are starting points. We need to ask such questions because if we don't understand the problem the product has to solve, we may be building the wrong solution and will not get the planned outcomes or benefits.

To fully understand the problem, various techniques and tools can be used at this stage, as explained below.

Gemba walks

Genba, known as Gemba, is a Japanese term which means 'actual place'. It has come to be associated with 'lean' management which normally relates to the manufacturing plant or the production flow. What Gemba simply means is that to understand the real problem, you must 'go and see'. In this way, you can observe what is happening in the actual working place, who does what and how. You can observe what they say, what they don't say, how they react to customers and the reaction of the customers in return etc. There is so much information which can only be collected via observation. This helps to get the full picture.

With Gemba walks you observe real problems which sometimes cannot be explained or revealed by formal methods like interviews or asking the customer. However, what is visible on the surface may not necessarily be a real problem. Hence it should be accompanied by multiple other techniques such as referencing data records, conducting field market research, interviews, working with people on the floor etc to identify possible problems.

These techniques allow researchers or the observer to find strategy related problems. So, at this stage, rather than just looking at one problem, many problems beneath the surface can be uncovered. Once the information is obtained, it is possible to move to the next stage of synthesizing the findings and converging.

D2 - Define the problem

At this stage, the data/research observations and interview results found at the D1 phase are synthesized to generate insights. Such insights help to discover the problem precisely. We use multiple tools in this phase and the common ones are personas and empathy maps.

Personas

A persona is a specific user of the product, rather than a generic user (a term which is broader in scope). For example, there is a difference between a 'customer' and 'Cindy'. It is more specific when you say 'Cindy, a 35-year-old, single mother who is on maternity leave'. Cindy has specific needs from the product which may not be required by John, who is a seventeen-year old high school rugby player. When you say 'user' Cindy's specific problems might not be captured. Cindy may be struggling with time. She may be going through a stressful situation with the new baby. Since she is a single mother, she may be feeling scared about the uncertainty of the future. So, what Cindy goes through is very specific problem compared to a generic 'user'.

Thus, persona can be a very powerful tool to identify the 'real problem' of a particular situation rather than what is visible on the surface. As an example, below is a persona of a consumer called Neil.

Motivation

James is an avid gamer and Twitch streamer studying game development in college. He is trying to find a niche for his Twitch channel, and is considering streaming some goofy VR games

Age: 19
Occupation: student, Twitch streamer
Family: away from home at college
Devices: Android, Gaming PC
Experience:
Virtual Reality

Goals

• find VR games that would be fun to stream
• draw viewers to channel w/ unique content
• see what's possible for beginner game dev

Figure 32: Persona of Neil

This persona is completely different from Cindy, as depicted above. They are different people and they may have completely different requirements or problems which your product needs to solve.

So, persona helps to identify different perspectives from different types of people. The product should interact with these different consumers to deliver value to them.

Empathy maps

Another powerful tool which can be used to synthesize the research findings is an empathy map. Empathy maps provide deeper insights into what the user (persona) says, thinks, does, and feels. They are powerful because sometimes people do not say the things they want to say. For example, people do not want to be impolite so will not say a product is a crappy product. Instead, their gestures hint that the product is no good. Take the example of a web page that takes longer than normal to load. As an example, I tap my fingers on the keyboard, very nervously and impatiently in such occasions. That gesture is a clear indication that I simply hate that this website takes such a long time to load the web page. But if someone asks me, I might not even remember to say that.

Below is a template of the empathy map which Product Owners can use to synthesis the findings relating to personas gathered from the D1 phase.

All these sessions and tools are highly collaborative. The more ideas you can get from different people, the more insights you will have. You should focus on collaborating with more people at both the D1 and D2 stages.

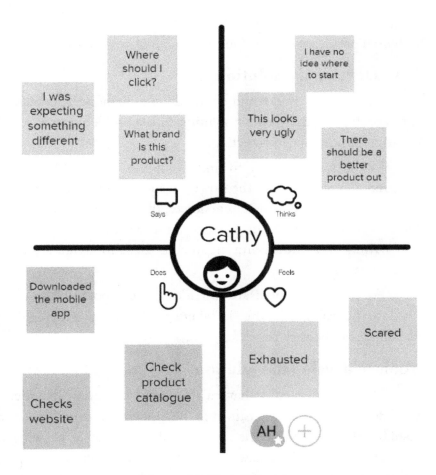

Figure 33: Empathy map

These sessions need to be organized properly and facilitated to achieve the results you need. The poster in Figure 33 above can be put up on a whiteboard. Provide an ample number of sharpies and post-it notes and guide the team to write down ideas/observations/insights section by section. Once the insights have been added to the poster, then as a group you can talk about them. Ask the team for details of the synthesis they came up with. Why might the users be saying that? Why do they think the user thinks like that? etc.

This exercise will lead to a summary of what the problem might be. Eventually, it will help you to narrow down a series of potential problems to a profound problem statement.

D3 - Develop the solution

In the second diamond of the double diamond approach, we focus on finding the possible solution to the problem statement we identified in the previous section.

When we are trying to find a solution to a problem, again, we cannot underestimate the power of ideation. What that means is that the more ideas we can generate, the more solutions we will have to solve the problem. Collaborating with many stakeholders and writing down ideas and organizing them to create a possible solution is essential.

At this stage, these are just ideas. These potential solutions need to be validated. This is where tools like prototyping and sketching can be very powerful.

Tools to develop the solution

We do not need to have a full-fledged solution in order to validate it. The solution can even be drawn on paper and then tested with the users. Tools like sketching; a kind of drawing on paper, can help to visualize the solution. Tools like prototyping; creating a mini model of the solution, can also be used for this.

I was once involved in developing a mobile app. We followed design thinking and wanted to make sure we were building the right product. So, instead of writing code and developing the mobile app in the computer, the team cut cardboard pieces into the shape and size of a mobile phone and used sharpies in different colors to draw the interface. For each screen, we created a cardboard piece. The investment to develop the solution was close to nothing. All we needed were cardboard boxes which we found in the mailroom. We did not even use computers or tools like photoshop to develop high fidelity user interfaces. It was so much fun and at the same time, everyone got involved. This is called prototyping.

We tested all the screens we developed on cardboard pieces with the real users who were people who visited the bank. It was fun for them too because instead of actual phones they were using cardboard pieces, but they got the idea. We were able to fine-tune the features required in the mobile app within only one week. We also saved money because if we had used the normal methodologies, like high fidelity computer representations, we might have had to get Adobe photoshop licenses or other tool licenses for the entire team. Also, we would not be able to achieve such high quality as collaboration would be close to zero. Team members would have been forced to work in a bubble on their own computers. The advantage of this method was that the entire team was now aware of the features and customers' reactions and preferences, so it was easy to develop at the development stage.

Prototyping and sketching are very powerful tools to identify potential solutions but there are also other tools which are highly effective at this step. We will discuss journey maps and story maps in detail later.

D4 - Deliver the solution

This is the step where we implement the solution we identified previously. To come to this stage, the potential solution identified in the previous steps needs to be iteratively tested with the customers/real users and then the final solution concept needs to be developed. At this stage, you should be able to say this is the problem and this is the solution due to this research data. At this stage you will identify the features required in the product. You will even know why some features need to be de-scoped because you will have tested those features with actual customers who gave negative feedback. You have data to back your decisions on the final solution or the final product.

Therefore, at this stage, you can begin to develop the product. The production process can be fast because the entire team has a very good understanding of what customers need, details of the product features and what value these product features will deliver to the customer.

This is the level where you, as the Product Owner, can create a product canvas, minimum viable product (MVP) to develop a high-level vision of the product. In addition to that, you also can create various artifacts like customer journey, product features, user stories, product backlog and user story mapping. We will discuss these in detail in the next chapter.

As you can see, design thinking helps to make customer-centric products. It reduces waste. It also engages all the users/customers/stakeholders at the very beginning of the process rather than keeping them waiting to the end without any clue of what is going on in the production house.

Design thinking can be applied to any type of product. It can be applied to technical products such as mobile apps as we discussed previously or Customer Relationship Management software etc. But it can be applied to non-technical products as well, for example, a workplace redesign product etc.

I have been involved in re-designing entire offices to make them more effective and enhance the productivity of employees. The old workplace resembled a box type workplace where everyone was separated. Employees did not even know the person next to them because they were in cubicles, separated by partitions.

We applied design thinking. The final design knocked down all the walls and partitions. This promoted discussion between employees from different departments. We planted huge trees in the middle of the floor and created a floor with real grass instead of tiles, adding greenery to the workplace. People sat on the grass like in a park. They would cross their legs and lean on a wall, keep their laptops on their laps and work. They sat on beanbags to work. We mounted ping pong tables and created mini-golf courses in the middle of the office. People loved it. They played games with people they did not even know before. This created a completely different culture where people loved to work because it was so relaxing. When coming to the office it was like going on an adventure or a holiday. It was also a very collaborative place.

Change management for products which use design thinking is minimal because the products are designed with the customer's collaboration. For the best results, design thinking should be used throughout the life of product development because products always need improvements and new features from time to time. Before applying any feature, it can be tested using the double diamond method to make sure it adds value to the user.

How to get the expertise

Design thinking is a special skillset. When applying design thinking it is necessary to understand the philosophy behind it. It involves various tools at different stages depending on the situation. Sometimes prototyping may not work. Practitioners should be able to decide which tool fits where. It also involves a lot of facilitation skills. The practitioner should be able to guide a user group to do ideation or prototyping. You need design thinking experts in these sessions.

Some companies bring an external consultant to facilitate product conceptualization at the beginning of product development. There is merit in doing that, however design thinking is something required throughout the product development process. Not only at the beginning. Hence you should think about a more sustainable solution.

Another approach is to have a design thinking expert on the

team. That can be a huge investment but if the product is a big product where multiple features are developed by many teams, this could be feasible. Also, if the product has a long life, getting the team trained on design thinking is highly effective as they can apply the techniques and tools throughout the life of the product. Such approaches are an investment but very effective.

At the end of the product conceptualization stage, you need to have a few artifacts developed before you move to the next stage of the real implementation of the product. One of the very important artifacts is the product canvas. Let's examine the product canvas in the next section.

Product canvas

One of the best ways to understand everything about the product is to create a product canvas. A product canvas helps to have a 360-degree view of the product. Starting from developing the product to delivering it and then earning money out of it can be explained using the product canvas. It can even be used to decide whether the product should be developed or dropped altogether. If there is no return on investment, there is no point in spending money.

Components of a product canvas

A product canvas covers the development and operational view of the product. To understand it better, let's look at the product canvas I created in order to develop the book you are reading right now.

This book is a product, and it needs to cover a lot of areas to deliver value to you as a reader. Just writing the book itself is not enough. To make it available to the reader, I have to do a lot of things. Hence, before I invested my time developing this product, I created the product canvas below to ensure this book is a viable product.

As you can see, developing a book as a viable product involves many components. This product canvas helped me to identify the key elements at the very beginning, before spending a single day writing. And it kept me thinking and working to bring it to a level where it could be a viable product.

Partners	Key Activities	Value Proposition	Customer Relationships	Customer Segments
Publishing Companies	Research on the market for other books	Knowledge sharing for the most demanding subject area	Website	Product Managers
Subject Matter Experts and peer reviewers	Structure the book	Helping people to build better career	Blog	Product Owners
Printing companies	Write	Building better products rightly	LinkedIn	Business Leaders
Delivery partners	Edit		Facebook	Agile Coaches
	Proofread		Direct Emailers	
	Peer Review			
	Publish			
	Market			
	Marketing			
	Selling			
	Track the sales and feedback			
	Follow-up on Feedback			
	Key Resources		**Channels**	
	Myself		Online commerce	
	Peers		Amazon	
	Proofreaders		Website	
	Book designers		Bookshops	
Cost Structure			**Revenue Streams**	
Delivery charges			Author royalty	
Labor (Key resources)				
Marketing				
eCommerce Setup				
Advertising				
Social Media subscriptions				

Figure 34: Product canvas

A product canvas can be divided into five main areas. It starts from the value of the product to be delivered to the customer (value proposition). The top-left corner lists what is needed to build the product. The bottom-left lists the costs. The top-right outlines the target market of the product and how to sell the product to the customer. The bottom-right forces you to think about how the revenue will be generated. Let us dig into more detail below.

Value proposition

What will the customer get when they buy this product? The value proposition is the heart of the product and of a business. Without value, the customer will not find the product appealing and will not buy it. Insights you derived in the first D of the double diamond will help you to identify the value customers are expecting from the product. If the value proposition cannot be articulated, that means it is still in the conceptual stage.

Key activities

Value is developed through a series of activities starting from conceptualization to delivering the product into the customers' hands. This section of the product canvas helps the Product Owner to think through and understand what activities are required to produce value. This 360-degree view of all the activities, before starting the production process, helps the Product Owner to understand various requirements like the different skills or external partners needed to develop the product.

Partners

Now that the Product Owner understands all the activities required to produce the product, he/she can then think about who is required to do these activities. Each activity needs a specialist with certain skills. It helps to think through who these people are (some call them `resources') and what skills they need.

Some of these resources may be available internally. If not, they will need to be sourced externally. For example, the product may require online transaction processing and this facility or technology may not be available internally. It may require getting a service provider such as PayPal.

Sometimes human resources may need to be found externally. For example, you might figure out you need a design thinking expert, but your company does not have any expertise in this area. In this case you could partner with a consultancy company or a recruitment agency to find the right skilled people.

Cost structure

Now that the Product Owner has identified everything and everyone needed to develop the product, the Product Owner can work on the cost structure. These are the costs associated with the product. It can be for the labor of the people who need to be hired or technology or infrastructure such as servers, software licenses, telecommunications, and even the rent for the office space.

When you list all the expenses you can even forecast how much it will cost to develop this product. This information will be required for a cost-benefit analysis of the product.

Customer segment

To whom are you going to sell this product? What is your market segment? This section of the product canvas allows you to think about the customer who will buy the product. In the double diamond discussed above, we identify the personas and ultimately these personas will be your customer segments.

Customer relationship

Once the customer segment is identified then the next step is figuring out how to engage with these customers. This step may be required even if the product is not yet ready. When we develop a product in an Agile way, we incorporate customers continuously in the production process. That improves the quality of the product by increasing the value and reducing the waste. You need to maintain a close connection with the customers.

This sometimes will incur some costs. For example, if you have to constantly update the customer, you may decide you need social media campaigns or CRM software. These will require licenses which add to the cost structure we discussed previously.

Channels

Once the product is ready, how do you intend to sell the product to the customer? How does the customer become aware of your product? How will the customer pay for the product? These are the questions you have to answer when you think about how to sell the product to the customer. What are the feasible channels available to sell the product once it is developed? Are you going to distribute it via distributors, or set up an e-Commerce site and put the product there? Or are you simply going to walk up to customers on the street and sell it that way?

Revenue streams

How are you going to get money from the product? That is the monetization part. Is it a subscription model? Or will the customer pay a license fee to use the product? Or are the distributors going to pay you money after they sell it to the customers? These are the different revenue streams that it is critical to think about before even developing the product. If you cannot articulate how you are going to make revenue out of the product then your investors will not be willing to spend money to develop it.

As you can see, the product canvas is precise and has all the necessary information you need before starting to develop the product on a large scale.

If you have been appointed as the Product Owner for an already determined product, that is if conceptualization has already been done, then you must ask for this product canvas. Chances are it may not exist. In that case, you must create the product canvas with the collaboration of everyone associated with the product, such as your team, stakeholders, sometimes with the customer as well. This will help to make sure everyone is on the same page regarding the product you are going to build.

Summary

When developing a product, the Product Owner must think about all the possible aspects such as competitor products, value proposition, sales channel, revenue channel etc. The product canvas is one of the tools which can help to get this 360-degree view of the product.

References

Ideo.com, 2015, design kit, The field guide to human-centered design, retrieved from Ideo.com

CHAPTER 7
JOURNEY MAPPING

In the product development process, another tool which may help is, journey mapping. A 'journey map', as indicated by its name, maps the end-to-end journey of a customer or employee (if it is an internal product). For ease of reference, we will refer to this tool as a 'customer journey map', but the concepts explained can be used even for employee or partner journey maps.

Customer journey mapping

Customer journey mapping is the technique which maps how customers use the product. What they do when they use the product, how they feel, their reaction, their emotions are all mapped to tell a story and generate insights.

The importance of mapping customer experience throughout the journey comes into the picture when we think of developing a product which customers love. If you know that customers are agitated using a product feature, that simply means that the customers' experience is not that great. If the customer is happy about using a specific feature, that is an area to dig deep into as well because if we understand why customers love that product feature it could be replicated and replace other product features customers do not like.

In this journey, the customer's experience can be mapped positively, neutrally, and negatively. Positive features should be kept, and the neutral and negative ones must be changed to provide a better customer experience end-to-end.

The customer journey can be created with a customer's

current product. The existing customer journey will give insights into what customers expect from the new product. Then based on this, what needs to be done to create that new journey can be developed.

Creating a customer journey is another collaborative session which requires engagement from all teams and if possible, the customers. The journey can be generated using research, data and insights gathered in D1 and D2 of the double diamond exercise we discussed in the previous chapter. Below is a customer journey map to purchase a product on an e-Commerce site.

Stage	Awareness	Consideration	Decision	Delivery	Use	Loyalty
Customer activities	Hear from friends, Facebook ads, Appear in Google search	Product quality, Price, Alternative products	Add items to shopping cart, Buy products from website	Track the order, Receive products	Use the product, Customer support for help	Repeat the orders, Promote the experience
Customer Goals	None	Find the best deal for the price	Easy product search, one click payment, zero transaction fee, save shopping cart	Receive the products within a short delivery delay	Good customer experience, Expect return on the investment	Save money, Save time,
Touch points	Word of mouth, social media	Word of mouth, social media, Google search,	Website, Mobile app, product reviews	Mobile app, website	Depends on the product, Phone	Social media, e-commerce website/app
Experience						
Business Goals	Reach many potential customers	Increase number of website visitors	Increase number of products, Increase shopping cart value, Influence customer to add more products	Get sales, Delivery on time, make customer returning customer	Receive product reviews, Return Customer returns to the site No product returns	Increase retention rate, Upsell, Turn customers to advocate
KPIs	Number of people subscribed, Number of people reached the call center, number of people visited the e-commerce site	New website visitors	Shopping cart value, Number of orders placed Number of abandoned carts	Customer rating, Revenue, Delivery time	Customer satisfaction rate, No of product returns	Number of customer returns, Number of customers dropped, number of new customer from advocates
Organizational activities	Create marketing campaigns Collect analytics Respond to queries	Reach the subscribed leads and offer the information requested, call back	Order processing, Promote other products Upselling Analytics recording Transaction processing	Delivery	Record reviews, Upselling	Customer support, Marketing
Responsible	Marketing Department, Customer service	Marketing department, Call center	Marketing, Logistics, Warehouse, IT	Delivery Partners, e-Commerce team, Delivery patterns	Marketing, Call center , Support Center	Marketing, Sales
Technology systems	CRM, Social media platforms, Google analytics	CRM, Google Analytics, Website analytics	CRM, e-Commerce Platform, Mobile app, PIM, Inventory system, Payment Gateway	Tracking system, e-Commerce site, Logistics system	IT helpdesk, Google analytics	Social Media, e-Commerce website/app, CRM

Figure 35: Customer journey map

Steps to create a customer journey map

- Identify the stages the customer must go through in the process. It is ok if the stages cannot be named properly, in that case, they can be left blank but identifying each step as a stage is important. List all the stages you identified at the top of the canvas.

- Identify the activities the customer would do at each of the stages. When you are creating a brand-new product, you can brainstorm on these activities. As an example, a customer would 'search for laptops.

- Then identify what 'touchpoints' a customer would use in each of these stages. As an example, where do they see the advertisements? How do they search for 'laptops'? Through which device, which system? For example, do they use Google or ask a friend, or do they walk to the nearest store and ask a shop assistant?

- Identify the customer goals at each of these stages. What do they intend to do or try to achieve at each stage? At the very first stage the customer may not have any specific goals. However, once they start searching for the product their goal may be to find more details about the product.

- Now, map their experience at each stage. If it is an existing product, your team must already know the customer experience at each stage as they will have done interviews and observations.

- Now map the business goals. At every stage, there must be a business goal. The business goal may be, for example, to increase brand awareness. You may expect that every visitor to the website is aware of the product you are selling. That is an expectation you have at that very first stage. This step will help you to be aware of any gaps in this area.

- Identify the organization's functional units, such as sales, marketing, or finance, which will be responsible for the internal operational work at each stage. For example, it is the job of the marketing division to increase brand awareness. If there is a gap in this area, the marketing team's collaboration will be required when the product is developed.

Sometimes it may not be clear who is responsible for the actions that need to be taken, but the team can brainstorm on which corporate function should be involved at each stage.

- Identify any Key Performance Indicators (KPI) to measure these activities or trends.

- Identify the manual or technical systems that it is necessary to use in each of these stages. For example, if it is the product returns stage, then the customer may have to engage with the existing customer portal. When you know which systems will be used, it helps you to understand which systems need to be updated or integrated to provide a better customer experience. If the Product Owner realizes that some systems do not exist, the Product Owner(PO) should think about how to implement or create integrations to make the product more feasible and valuable.

As you can see, the customer journey provides a 360-degree view of the product. It helps to find out how the customer interacts with the product and the experience of the customer at each of those stages. Journey mapping is a good exercise to figure out the minimum viable and minimum marketable products. And it also helps to identify everything which needs to be developed to make a valuable product rather than only focusing on product development.

Summary

Customer Journey Mapping is a powerful tool which can be used to understand customer experience from the beginning to the end of the product use. It helps to map each stage of the product use, the experience at each stage and associated internal activities. This tool gives an indication as to which areas of the product have problems and possible causes of the negative experience.

CHAPTER 8
PRODUCT BACKLOG

The product backlog is one of the main artifacts that you must develop before you begin product development. If you don't have a product backlog you are not ready to start. Not only that, if you don't have a product backlog, you have not done your job properly either.

The product backlog is everything which needs to be done to develop the product and then ship the product to the consumers. The consumers may be employees belonging to the company you work for or they may be external customers who purchase the product.

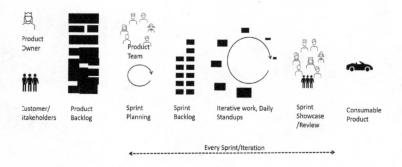

Figure 36: Product backlog

The product backlog lists all the product features the product should have. The insights needed to create the product backlog come from the D1 and D2 activities, along with personas, the product canvas, the customer journey map and empathy maps, all of which we have seen in previous chapters. Items in the product backlog should be implemented to make the product usable and valuable to the customer. It will take weeks and months and sometimes years to implement all the items listed in the product backlog.

Imagine the product backlog like a storeroom. The Product Owner and the team can put many things into the storeroom. These items are the requests from different people/parties such as customers, stakeholders, partners, suppliers, team members and Product Owner(PO)s. Various people/parties can request additions to the product, but the decision will be with the Product Owner(PO). The Product Owner will decide whether to implement those requests or not.

Items in the product backlog should be taken out and should be built as the product. So, over a period of time, ideally, the product backlog should be emptied. But sometimes, some items in the backlog may not be implemented at all.

The Product Owner owns the product backlog. It is his/her territory and he/she decide what to do with the items in the product backlog. Should they be materialized as the product or not? When should they be materialized? Sometimes the Product Owner decides some items should be materialized immediately, like within the next two weeks; some are not so urgent and can wait; and some items are not required at all.

These decisions should be very informed with a clear rationale as various people/parties have an interest in seeing these items in the product. For example, the finance division says that all the commodities sold on the e-Commerce site should be in compliance with trade regulations. They expect compliance to be enforced immediately. If the Product Owner decides not to implement this item then he/she has to give a clear rationale to the finance division.

Even if the Product Owner owns the product backlog, the Product Owner shouldn't be a dictator. Decisions should be made with information and data, with a proper rationale so that product stakeholders, consumers and the team can understand why an item will or will not be implemented. We call this product backlog prioritization. The product features are prioritized with a proper balance to make the best product available to all the parties.

Composition of the product backlog

The backlog consists of various items. It consists of foundational or architectural components, product behaviors or features the product should offer, and everything else which needs to be done to launch the product to the market.

Each Agile framework classifies these items differently so there will be multiple terminologies, but most of the time they refer to the same concept. The Product Owner can adopt the terminology of the framework which he/she is used to operating. However, let's first try to understand the concepts, before we get into the confusing world of terminologies.

Epics, features, and user stories

Basically, the product backlog consists of epics, features, and user stories. Let's say you are building a house. Epics will be the larger items like the landscape garden, swimming pool, ground floor, rooftop garden etc. Each of these larger items has some behaviors which can be treated as features. For example, the swimming pool has a warm and cold-water treatment feature, or it might have a sauna area feature. It has an automatic cleaning system and a motion-controlled lighting system. Each of these features can be further divided into smaller value delivery items called a 'user story'. As an example, the user of the swimming pool may want to control the water flow. This user story is part of the warm and cold-water treatment feature, in addition to other items which make up this feature. The entire product can be divided into epics, features and user stories.

Let's take another example using a software product. Let's say you are developing an e-commerce product which is an e-commerce website and a mobile app. The e-Commerce website will be an epic.

Also, the mobile app is an epic. Each epic should be able to be explained by its intended features and the benefits of implementing it.

Features

As we saw above, epics can be divided into features. Product features are in-built in the product and directly part of the product. These features may be tangible, as well as intangible. For example, a product catalogue, product pricing, a shopping cart, the customer order history, promotional campaigns, and the search facility are all part of an e-Commerce website.

Each epic can be divided into many features depending on the details of the information identified. However, it is always good practice to identify the return on investment of implementing a feature. Like epics, features are also significant investments in terms of time, money and effort, so perhaps it will not be possible to implement all the features identified. As an example, consider the sauna area we discussed in the previous section. Is it really required? What is the cost-benefit or return on investment of implementing a sauna area associated with the swimming pool? To decide that, you can do a cost-benefit analysis for each product feature.

Below are a few features and their benefits for the epic e-Commerce website.

Feature	Benefit
The saved shopping cart of the customer	Improved customer experience and increasing click to cash cycle time of the customer (customer can repeat the order without searching for new products)

Video product demonstration of the products	Reduce the product returns by providing precise information on the product before purchase Increase customer confidence buying the product Increase the number of sales
Cash on delivery payment method	Increased customer segment of those who don't have or use credit cards Reduce the transaction fees payable to payment processors

Epics, enablers, and features give you a very good understanding of what the product will be like when it is built. However, since we are moving towards real implementation or the development, we can further break down features into a more detail-oriented version called user stories.

User stories

High-level details are not enough to plan product development. A micro-level is also necessary. User stories provide that detailed version.

Features can be divided into user stories. A user story, as the name suggests, and as we have discussed in a previous chapter, is specific to different users. The product you develop needs to be used by different people with different personas. Each persona has a different requirement and different use for the product. Let's take the feature 'product video demonstration' as an example.

'Demo of the product' is used by multiple users as depicted in the figure below.

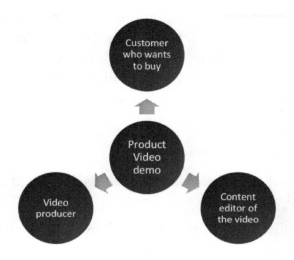

Figure 37 : Same feature but different stories

Each of these users has different requirements from this feature. Although it is the same video, the way the three users use this product feature will be quite different and will have different requirements. Unless the Product Owner considers all the users associated with the feature and provides the functionality they expect, the product is not going to add value for all users.

So, the Product Owner should consider what user stories are associated with each product feature. As an example, a user who wants to buy an air fryer which is sold via the e-Commerce site you are going to build has a story like the following;

> As a housewife (the customer who wants to buy an air fryer)
>
> I want to see how the air fryer works before buying
>
> So that I can see if it does not use oil at all.

But for the content editor who must constantly create videos and upload them to the e-Commerce site, his/her story is very different. The content editor's job is to stitch the video clips to make new ones, and probably split the videos into small segments of frames, and then add audio or change the audio, add video searchable meta tags etc. So, his/her story relevant to the same video should look like the following;

> As the content editor
>
> I want to fragment the video to frames, edit the audio and add meta tags to the video
>
> So that I can create videos even from the archived videos.

As you can see, two different users have completely different requirements from the same product features. Unless you consider all these users it will be less valuable to other users. So, once you identify the product epics and features you must break these down into smaller units, the user stories.

User stories should be written with the user as the focus point. They can be written using the format below.

> As the [User name]
>
> I want to [expected activity or function]
>
> So that [benefit].

User stories are more applicable when the product moves into the development phase. To facilitate the process, there are a few guidelines when writing user stories. We normally call this an INVEST approach.

INVEST approach to writing user stories

Independent

User stories are independent so that they can be implemented independently without any conjunction with other user stories.

Negotiable

User stories are not a contract. They are negotiable. The details of the user story may be fine-tuned as the team progresses and the original user story does not need to be implemented as it is. The team and the Product Owner should be able to negotiate the details and make the commitments accordingly.

Valuable

User stories should always deliver some value. Tangible or intangible. If the value it delivers is not comprehensible or explainable then either the user story needs to be fine-tuned or the user story should not be implemented.

Estimable

A user story should be able to be estimated using the chosen estimation techniques. Some teams use Fibonacci story points (e.g. 1, 2, 3, 5, 8, 13, 20 etc.) and some teams use hours and days. Whatever the method the teams use, the stories should be able to be estimated.

Small

User stories should be small enough so that they can be estimated. If a user story is large, like 100 story points, or takes twenty days, the user story should be split into smaller ones. It should be small enough to fit into an iteration or a sprint. As an example, if the team is on a two-week (ten days) sprint, then the user story should be small enough to fit into ten days iteration. If not, then it needs further splitting.

Testable

The user story should be able to be tested in the sprint itself. That means criteria to say 'yes it meets the expected quality of this user story' should be clear. So, the question is: What are the expected quality needs to be discussed (negotiated)? The team needs to be clear about the acceptable criteria so they can be implemented from day 1. If the team or Product Owner are not clear about this, either the user story is not clear enough or it is complex so some discussion is necessary to drill down the details. Or else, it needs to be split into smaller user stories.

So, as you can see, the product backlog can consist of epics, enablers, features and user stories. All these have a different level of details. Epics and enablers are at a high level, but the user stories consist of granular level details.

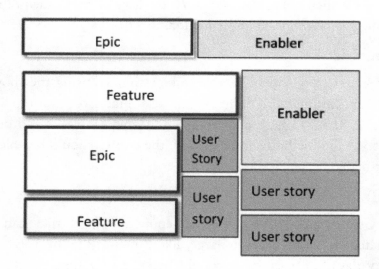

Figure 38: Composition of product backlog

Acceptance criteria

In the process of writing user stories, the next step is to understand the acceptance criteria. Acceptance criteria create a fine balance between desirability and feasibility. Desirability is the user's expectation from the user story. Feasibility is what is implementable within the team's constraints. For example, the customer may like to have 4K video quality. However, the team says 4K video production requires special cameras to record the video and high-end software to process the videos. This equipment and software are not available due to budgetary constraints. So the Product Owner and the team reach a middle ground. It will not be 4K quality, but it at least needs to have high definitions above 720 pixels and should have subtitles.

Acceptance criteria are a sort of quality criteria which need to be met when the product is developed. Without acceptance criteria, the team will struggle in the development phase. You, as the Product Owner, would say 'No this is not acceptable quality' and the team would respond 'Well we did not know what quality you were expecting'. This will lead to waste and rework. It will make the development process longer and the Product Owner will not be able to release the product to the customer as promised. So, to avoid all this drama, it is a must that the team and the Product Owner discuss the acceptance criteria at the time the user stories are written.

Product backlog development and collaboration

As we have discussed, the product backlog is conceptual storage where the product exists in the form of epics, enablers, features, and user stories. Once these are implemented, the real product will emerge. Hence the creation of the product backlog with the necessary details is, in itself, an achievement. However the Product Owner cannot create the product backlog on his/her own. If this happens, it will not be the full representation of the product. Collective brainpower is critical for creating a comprehensible product backlog.

Product backlog items such as epics and enablers need high-level details, while features and user stories need low-level details. You, as Product Owner, may not have technical background and may not be able to add any technical limitations. As an example, I (the author) personally have no idea about different video qualities in order to be able to say that a video is good quality above 720 pixels. I had to ask a videographer to explain it and if I didn't ask questions, I may not have got the right level of details. A Product Owner may have even more complicated situations. After creating the product backlog, the Product Owner(PO) will update the CEO or sponsor (who finances the product development) saying that the videos they produce will be high quality and they may assume it will be like 4K. But the truth is your team does not have the capabilities to create such high-end quality videos. So, if you don't understand the details then you will be providing wrong commitments to the leaders and customers. So, you must ensure you get the right level of details.

Such work needs collaboration with all the levels associated with the products. Even the customers, when possible. Business functions such as finance, logistics, supply chain, marketing and sales, along with technical teams such as solution architects, enterprise architects, software engineers, testers, production support, IT operations etc. all need to contribute to developing the product backlog.

Hence, organizing this event is paramount. To organize and run the event, the Product Owner needs a lot of help from a few people. The sponsor of the product may need to support this event, especially if it requires some budget. It needs to be a collaborative workplace, with everyone in one room, face-to-face. People may need to fly over if they are in different geographical locations. It sounds costly, but in fact, it is an investment to build the product right away.

The Product Owner should get help from the Agile coach or a senior Scrum Master to organize and run the session. Having a design thinking expertise is required to create a customer journey.

This event should take place before the product starts development or production. We always recommend having a session called 'Discovery' which can last a week to four weeks depending on the complexity of the product and the scale. Then within that discovery, two days can be dedicated to creating the product backlog where everyone should be co-located and co-creating.

In this collaboration, the Product Owner should not forget to involve suppliers, vendors and partners who are external to the Product Owner's company. Everyone should be co-located and at the end of the two days, the full product backlog should be created. Hence the event needs to be planned and guided to get the desired outcome.

Such events are perfect for product development when it starts full-fledged development. Once we create the product backlog, the next thing we need to figure out is how to organize all these features in a way that will give maximum value to the customer. This is where we need to examine the concept of 'minimal viable product'.

Minimum viable product (MVP)

Customers need the product/solution you are developing to solve a problem, so the sooner they have the product, the better. They expect the product to be available for them urgently, if possible, the next day. But when we look at our product backlog, the epics, features and user stories cannot be developed or implemented immediately. It will take some time. Sometimes it may be a few weeks, sometimes it may be a few years. It all depends on the complexity and the availability of the skills, resources etc. But customers do not like to wait. They need the products to be available soon so you, as the Product Owner, need to find a way to respond to this urgency. How about providing a product which can be developed quickly but is still usable by the customer? That is the concept of the minimum viable product (MVP).

When developing an MVP, you need to be incredibly careful. It is not about delivering any old thing because it can be developed by the team immediately. It should not be like the figure below.

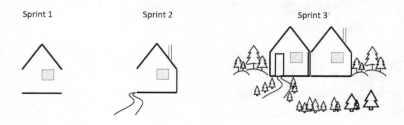

Figure 39: Wrong way to do MVP

It may be easy and quick to develop and deliver, but it cannot be used. The customer does not get any value out of that. Hence the Product Owner needs to collaborate with the customer, suppliers, partners and team and decide which list of epics, features, user stories are feasible to develop and deliver as soon as possible while still being valuable to the customer. So, it will be something like the figure below.

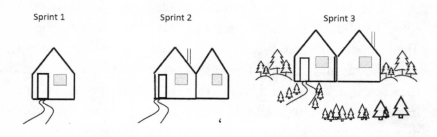

Figure 40: Right way to do MVP

That means the product is developed incrementally, but at the end of every increment a usable, desirable product feature/features is/are implemented and given to the customer. When it is done in this manner, the customer can still use the product, and you as an organization get an incremental revenue. So, this is a way to increase the return on investment rather than asking the customer to wait until the full product is developed.

So you must identify the minimal viable product and plan development accordingly. But wait. Don't forget the commercial aspects of the product. Is the MVP acceptable to your sales team? To your marketing team? Will they support you to market the product increment? This is where we need to discuss the concept of the minimal marketable product (MMP).

Minimum marketable product (MMP)

The minimum marketable product is the other concept we need to consider when we talk about making the product commercially available. Think about a product like Apple iPhone which is launched globally. MVP itself may not be sufficient to market a branded, high profile product like iPhone. It needs a few extras to make it a successful, marketable product. As an example, the packaging. Apple is renowned for its packaging concepts. When you receive the product in your hands, you feel like you have received something special. People never thought about these things before. But Apple proved that packaging plays an important role. It is sleek, simple, aesthetic, and you do not even feel like throwing it away. So, this packaging is something that goes with the MVP. In addition, the user manual, after sales service, warranties and customer support are all essential components of the product when it is launched.

The other components that need to be considered are marketing and advertising, change management activities, operational readiness and after-sales support (such as call center integration etc.). The integration of these functions needs other teams' involvement and may be even costly. For example, the marketing team may advise you that launching marketing campaigns are expensive so, it may not be economical to do these very frequently. Collaboration and negotiation with other functions are necessary to make the product available to the market. These are the components of a product experience.

But how does the Product Owner decide which epics, enablers, features, and user stories should be included in the MVP and MMP? For that purpose, the customer journey mapping we discussed earlier, which includes touchpoints and what business functions should be involved, should be considered.

....

NOW LET'S move on to another section of the discovery with the next level of details. With each of these steps, we are moving from the macro-level of the product conceptualization towards more micro-level details as we are planning and getting ready to begin product development.

Once we have the customer journey, minimum viable product, and the full backlog with the epics, features, and user stories, we need to properly select the user stories needed to deliver the MMP of the product. We do this with a product road map.

Product road map

With the product backlog, you get the volume, quality, and the scope of the product. But with the product roadmap, we add a time dimension, that is, how long will it take to develop the product. The Product Owner needs to be able to answer questions like, 'When will the product be available on the market? When can I start using the product? When will this issue be resolved?'

We previously discussed that the customer expects the product to be available soon, while the business leaders also need the product to generate its target revenue or benefits. But to do that, the MVP and MMP need to be developed and you have limited resources for that, and it takes time.

In the previous section, we saw that the product backlog consists of several hundred user stories. The Product Owner has a limited number of people to do everything. This is where the incremental development organized around the product roadmap is very useful. The product roadmap explains the development timeframes at a high level and what to expect in each of the product subsets.

Contents of a product roadmap

The product roadmap consists of a few integral components. The first is the timeline. When deciding the timeline, it is necessary to understand the concept of time boxing.

Time boxing is the concept of 'fixing' the timelines and then 'selecting the scope to fit the time box'. As an example, you may remember we discussed having standups and it is 'time boxed' for fifteen minutes. Similarly, you have to decide when to release the products/product features to the customer. However, we should remember that the customer needs the product quickly and other aspects need to be considered like market trends and big events coming up.

Special events like Thanksgiving, Christmas, Easter, or New Year are the times when there is a boost in sales for some products. So, if you are developing an e-Commerce product, launching it just after Christmas may not yield any returns for you or any value to the customer. Instead, if you launch it just one month before the peak period, you can assess its performance and adjust anything as required to make it ready for the peak period. Your timeline should be based on insights from external events, and the capacity available within the team to develop the decided MVP and MMP.

The Product Owner may come up with a roadmap like the

following:

When	Quarter 1 (March)	Quarter 2 (June)	Quarter 3 (Sep)	Quarter 4 (Dec)
Release/Version Name	Spring	Summer	Fall	Winter
Goal				
MMV features	List of features	List of features	List of features	List of features
Metrices				

Figure 41 : Sample product roadmap

The Product Owner may also decide to release a lightweight version of the MVP for initial milestones, with more features to be added later, depending on what is learnt from the first release. As an example, in the e-Commerce product, you may decide to go with the cash on delivery feature in the first release without integrating any payment gateways like PayPal. Integrating PayPal requires more R&D and operational readiness and would make the 'time to market' longer.

You can then identify how the Product Owner can measure the goal once implemented. For example, it can be the number of orders placed, the number of new customer registrations etc.

Once created, the product roadmap can be made available to all the parties involved so that they all share the same goal. The product roadmap needs to be developed with the collaboration of multiple parties, so everyone has ownership. Different teams may focus on a small segment of the product backlog but they all should share the same goal. Unless all teams deliver on time and integrate all the work into one product, the product cannot be released.

When	Quarter 1 (March)	Quarter 2 (June)	Quarter 3 (Sep)	Quarter 4 (Dec)
Release/ Version Name	Spring	Summer	Fall	Winter
Goal	Introduce the online shopping to the region			
MMV features	Web version 100 products Cash on delivery Operations in one country	Mobile version iOs 500 products integration Sprint version 1+ Postal delivery 1 country	Mobile version Android Web+iOS versions 5000 products 3rd party dealer integration for delivery 1 country	List of features Fall features + All products APAC region
Metrices	10k customer visits 1000 Orders placed 100K revenue Less than 100 returns	1 million customer visits 5K app downloads 200K revenue <1000 returns	2 million customer visits 5K app downloads 500K revenue <1000 returns	5 million customer visits 10K app downloads 1Million revenue <100 returns

Figure 42 : Sample product roadmap for an e-Commerce product

User story mapping

Once the product roadmap is determined and agreed then it is necessary to prioritize the product backlog based on the delivery milestones. A decision needs to be made as to which product features are required for the first product version and what associated user stories are required to do that. This is done through the user story mapping explained below.

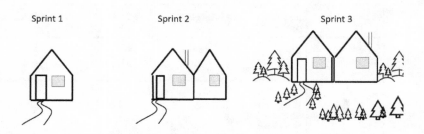

Figure 43 : Iteration 1 product features

As per the product roadmap, your first version may be like the figure above. In that case, what are the user stories required to create the first version of the product? You and your team need to collaborate and pick the features and user stories, as below, for development.

Once the team does that, the user stories belonging to release 1 should be developed starting from the first sprint.

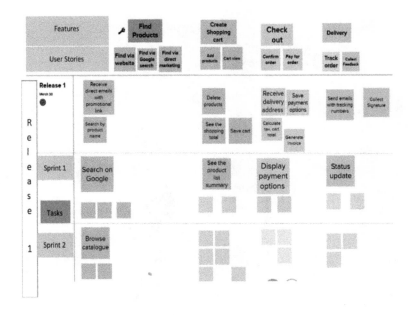

Figure 44: Story mapping of an e-Commerce version 1

Summary

Preparation to develop a product involves various artifacts. Macro and micro level thinking and planning are necessary. Decisions need to be made about what product features are needed down to very fine details, such as performance of the product. Various tools come to the rescue during this process and a good Product Owner knows which tool/artifact to use, when and for which purpose.

References

NBC News wire services and Paul A. Eisenstein, 2012, Toyota to hold world's biggest car recall in 16 years, retrieved from nbsnews.com

CHAPTER 9
DEVELOPING THE PRODUCT

Now that the Product Owner has identified most of the big-ticket items such as the product backlog and the product roadmap, it is to time to start the production or the development process. Now the team needs to get involved with the details as they are going to develop the items in the product backlog. When I say the team here, I refer to all the teams, including the launch and commercial teams.

This is where the teams will really use the Agile method of working. It may be one team or multiple teams, and everyone will follow the Agile process we discussed previously. They will follow the regular cadence of sprint planning, daily standups, backlog refinement, sprint showcase and retrospective. If the product is developed by multiple teams, then there will be inter-team synchs, called Scrum of Scrums and Solutions Demo, where product pieces built by multiple teams will be integrated.

Each team works on completing a specific scope within a short period of the sprint. This specific scope is the 'sprint backlog'. A sprint backlog is the subset of scoping items which has been picked from the product backlog and the team commits to execute this within the identified time box period of the sprint/iteration. That means items in the sprint backlog should be completed within the sprint duration. To make things simple, we will assume the sprint duration is two weeks. Let's examine what the sprint backlog should consist of.

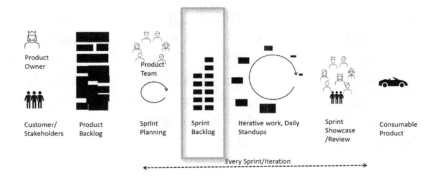

Figure 45: Sprint backlog

Sprint backlog composition

During the sprint planning, the Product Owner and the team will pick the list of user stories to be part of the sprint backlog. They will use the priority the Product Owner has set up in the product backlog. That means the team will select the user stories from the top of the product backlog. For example, all the user stories belonging to the next immediate release as per the product road map would be at the top of the product backlog. The team will pick the user stories to fit their two-week capacity.

Normally at the very beginning (before the sprint planning session), the sprint backlog will just be a list of user stories. But during the sprint planning, the team will split these user stories into tasks. Some of these user stories will be explorations like technical spikes (such as checking if they can use machine learning (ML) to generate customer behaviors). Some of the user stories will address technical debt. As an example, the team has realized that the system is slow due to the way the code has been previously written. Now they have figured out a way to rewrite the code so that the code runs much faster. So that is an improvement, but they do need to rewrite the previous code to get the full benefits.

This is called refactoring. They can keep it as a lower priority. But if they proceed without rewriting it, it will be more difficult in the future as they will be adding more and more code, which makes it extremely difficult to disentangle. (I use the analogy of a tangled hair to explain this. The longer you keep it, the more difficult it is to disentangle it.) Hence the sprint backlog may include improvement user stories identified by the team, even though these have not been identified by the Product Owner.

Figure 46: Technical debt

If the product is already in use by customers/users, then they might have reported some issues, defects or bugs. As an example, let's say an e-Commerce website is already up and running and used by thousands of customers. A few customers have reported when they pay using a credit card that they have not been issued with an invoice. This issue now needs to be first analyzed and then fixed and provided with an immediate production release so that future transactions will not have the same issue. This was not in the product backlog, but it just came up as a result of customer feedback. It needs immediate action as it is illegal not to issue invoices when the payment is made by the customers. Such bug fixes need to be included in the sprint backlog.

That means the sprint backlog will include different types of user stories from different sources such as product backlog, the team, other teams such as operations and customer support and external customers. Its composition resembles the figure below.

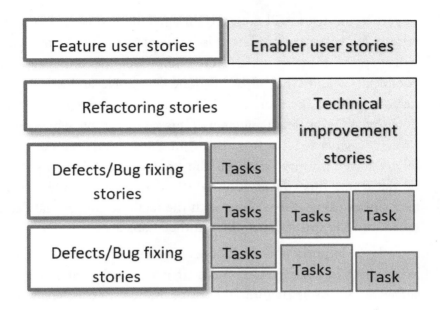

Figure 47: Composition of sprint backlog

These user stories, enabler stories, improvement stories, and tasks have different complexities, uncertainties and dependencies. The team will factor in these knowns and unknowns when they measure the size of the user stories. To understand the complexities, uncertainties and expectations, the team can work on three Cs during the sprint planning session.

Card, Conversation and Commitment (3Cs)

In an Agile environment, we write the user stories on an index card. The user story is written on the front side and on the back, we write the acceptance criteria. The Product Owner needs to provide guidance in terms of the acceptance criteria, but the Product Owner does not know everything. It is therefore necessary to have a conversation for each user story.

This is a group conversation with the team members, Scrum Master and the Product Owner. Questions can be asked, and knowledge can be shared which will help to understand the details.

Together the team will come to an agreement on the acceptance criteria for when the user story is implemented. This conversation will help the team to use collective knowledge to understand the complexities and what must be done to resolve and identify the necessary tasks. The user story is split into tasks which need to be done by different team members. This conversation will help the Product Owner to learn from the team. Sometimes user stories may take a lower priority based on the knowledge or insights shared by the team. This conversation will lead to estimating the size of user stories using story points, with the team deciding what can be taken into the sprint depending on their capacity.

It is important that Product Owners trust that the team knows best in their specific fields. If it is a technical subject like software or infrastructure, the team knows best. They operate with the resources they have. When freedom, motivation and a purpose are provided, they will always do their best to make the best product, it is in their interests too. It's true that the Product Owner is aware of the big picture: the priority, product road map and sometimes the investments made to build the product. But if the Product Owner tries to challenge the team asking them why they cannot take more and more work, he/she will be doing harm. When Product Owners try to put more pressure on teams, the team will compromise on quality. Hence, as a Product Owner, your job is to give them the necessary clarity and build an environment where they will be empowered to decide the best way to implement user stories.

Once this conversation takes place and details are clarified, the team will pick user stories which they can commit to within the two-week sprint. The whole team tells the Product Owner which user stories they can commit to (sprint scope) and the Product Owner agrees. If there are any user stories which are large and cannot fit in the current sprint or details are not sufficient so a commitment cannot be made, these user stories will go back into the product backlog. The Product Owner must work on obtaining enough details to implement those user stories which are lacking information.

User story mapping can be used as a way to organize the user story split and tasks in the sprint backlog as follows.

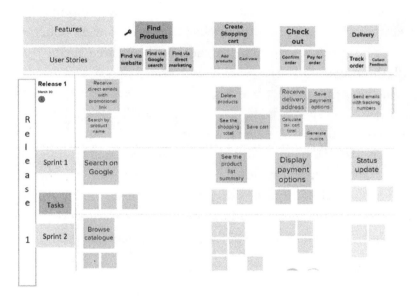

Figure 48: User story breakdown

What happens to the sprint backlog during the sprint?

Items in the sprint backlog start getting emptied during the sprint. Daily, the team picks items from the sprint backlog and starts developing them.

During the development process the team also will identify some other tasks that they will add into the sprint backlog. So, the sprint backlog can get new items. However, if the new item is, say, a big user story and the team cannot commit to it, then the Product Owner needs to put that item back into the product backlog.

Towards the end of the sprint, items in the sprint backlog

should be almost finished, unless some new tasks were added by the team. Hence it is a gradual decrement.

Synchronizing the work done by multiple teams

Depending on the complexity of the product, the product may have multiple sprint backlogs. That is, depending on the number of teams involved in the product development. As an example, let us say the product has three Agile teams operating in the same cadence. That means there will be three sprint backlogs. All three sprints backlogs will pick the features and user stories from the same product backlog. However, Product Owners of each sprint should synchronize their work to make sure all of them are up to date on what is happening with each sub-team. That will also help to discover each team's dependencies. So, the Product Owners of each team should meet at regular intervals, daily if possible, for a short period of time in order to update each other. This can be like the daily standups for the teams. As this is a meeting between Product Owners, we can call this a Product Owner's standup.

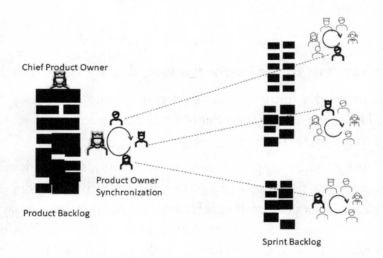

Figure 49: Product Owner synchronization

Summary

During product development, many actions become critical. This is when the product backlog needs to be re-planned and prioritized based on feedback from the customers, team and stakeholders. A product backlog should always be up to date and consist of product features, technical features and improvement or innovation tasks.

CHAPTER 10
PRODUCT OWNER'S ACTIVITES DURING THE DEVELOPMENT

In this section, we will discuss the Product Owner's responsibilities during each phase of the product life cycle.

- During conceptualization

- During production

- During the disposal

Since the focus is on using the Agile methodology, relevant events in the Agile process will be used throughout this section.

1 During product conceptualization	2	3

In this section, we will assume that the Product Owner has already been selected internally or hired and has been asked to lead the specific product development. Below are the Product Owner's responsibilities during this phase. This is just a summary. Please refer to the previous chapter for details.

Clarify the Product Owner's role

Do not start with assumptions. You may have thought that you understood the role, but management may have a different view. Do this even before the conceptualization phase or as soon as you are appointed as the Product Owner.

Clarify your role, responsibilities, expectations and how you will be measured in your job. Product management is a serious business. An organization's future may be dependent on the product you are about to develop. The Product Owner is part of the organization's growth so understand exactly what is expected of you.

To whom do you report? Who is your go-to person if required? Who has the details about the strategy and what is the strategy? The people who hired you may not have even thought about these questions. But when you ask these questions, that will help them to realize that all of this is part of your job as well.

You should be equipped with everything necessary for success. If you fail, the strategy of the organization will also fail. Hence the required support should be made available to you on this journey. Ask the questions and get clarification before you move forward.

Understand the Product Owner's authority

As a Product Owner, you have the authority to decide many things, as we discussed in the previous chapters. But unless you are the owner of a startup or developing your own product, you do not have full authority. Hence, understand what the limits of your authority are, when to seek approval and how.

Understand the strategy, why this product is required

Don't move forward without knowing how your product fits into the strategy. The biggest failures in product development occur when you develop a product without even knowing why the product is needed. This can confuse everyone, including the leaders. The real connection to the strategy might only be realized when the money has been wasted without any returns.

When the Product Owner understands the strategy and how the product will help to achieve the organization's goals, then it is very easy to get motivated and motivate the team as well. In this case everyone feels like they have a role in shaping the future of the company.

Understanding the strategy will also help you to decide if you want to have a long discovery session or not. If there is no such strategy, then you can even get the leaders into the discovery room and figure out the bigger problem that they want you to solve.

Understand the boundaries of the Product Owner role

What are the systems and products your product should interact with? Who are the owners of those products? If you want information or modifications to upstream and downstream systems, what is the process and who should you contact? What dependencies does your product have and what systems depend on your product?

Do you have the authority to release the product when you want, or do you have to follow an enterprise release cycle? Those are things you must be aware of before even moving into product development.

Understand the stakeholders

Who are the people you must work with? Who are the vendors and suppliers your product needs input from or needs to provide output to?

What are the other business divisions, for example finance, supply chain, IT, human resources, that you need information from and should provide information to? Sometimes these divisions may be directly involved with the product, whereas sometimes it may be indirect involvement. For example, if an e-Commerce product needs to be integrated with the supply chain, then the supply chain system must develop application programming interfaces (APIs) to integrate with your e-Commerce product. So you need their support.

The Product Owner needs to establish a very good relationship with the other divisions involved. He/she should have face-to-face conversations to discuss the plan and communication methods etc. This is one of the main actions a Product Owner should take before starting product development.

Understand the skills required to build the product

What skills are required to build the product? Do you have a team with all these skills? If not, then how do you find people with the right skills? Can you hire them from internal teams? What if those skills are not internally available? Then the Product Owner may have to get help from a consultancy company who can provide those skilled people. Or else maybe outsourcing is an option.

The Product Owner must figure this out at the very early stage of product development because you need the team even for the discovery level of the product. Without them, you will not be able to create the product backlog and the other elements we discussed in previous chapters.

Structure the team

Once the hiring part is done, establish the team structure. Identify the Scrum Masters, architects, UX designers, software engineers etc. If the product is a large one which needs multiple teams, then split the team to create a few small teams.

The product should not move forward without Scrum Masters. With the Agile methodology it is mandatory to have a Scrum Master for each team. Likewise, you must have a Product Owner for each team. If there is just one team, then you will be the Product Owner. But if you have multiple teams, you need to appoint Product Owners for the other teams as well.

Get to know the team and kick off team bonding sessions

Your team is one of the big pillars of the success of the product. Without a great team, the Product Owner may not be able to build the best possible product.

The product team will be diverse with different skills. They might even come from different cultural backgrounds. They may have different seniorities. This is the time to get to know them. Help them to be self-organized. 'When we can build a great team, we can do great things.'

Organize logistics

Where is the product team going to sit? What tools do they need? Do they have mobile phones to communicate? Do they have laptops or workstations? Do they need video conferencing facilities to connect with members in other locations? Do they have enough stationary? How will they get home if they work late hours? Do they have access to cafes? Do they need snacks? Or even a ping pong table? Do they need a place to take a nap (yes a nap!). Remember we are not talking about the traditional way of working. What's wrong with them taking a nap if they are tired?

All these are the questions a good leader asks (if they are a Product Owner, a coach or a Scrum Master). You need to prepare your workplace. When your team needs energy, your office should provide them with the snacks and food they need. When Agile is properly implemented, the workplace transforms into a dynamic space. Developing products with Agile is very different from the traditional way of working and you need to be ready for that.

Organize a regular cadence to get going

You may not have even started properly but at least you have been appointed and you have a few team members. So, you should get the rhythm going.

Get help from the Scrum Master to create a proper cadence with weekly planning, stand-ups, Kanban walls and retrospectives at the end. From day one these should be implemented so that the team gets familiar with the way they are going to work.

Organize a discovery session

This needs to be done even before the product development starts. (We discussed the details of this session in a previous chapter.)

At the end of the discovery session, the Product Owner can get into the high-level details of the product and clarify assumptions, dependencies and risks that he/she needs to deal with.

Organize necessary training

In the previous chapters, we talked about various new tools and methodologies your product team will use. Some of these are design thinking, Agile, DevOps, communication strategies, along with collaboration tools like Microsoft Teams, Jira etc. You need to organize training for the team and other stakeholders, partners and suppliers as well. Do not assume they are all comfortable using these tools and methodologies. Even if they are, your team will be using them in a unique way with your product. So, start at level zero. Let everyone gain familiarity with them and it will help to improve team productivity.

Establish the communication strategy

Communication is one of the key factors in product management. There are so many integral components and parties to be kept updated. As your product is linked to the strategy, leaders want to know how the product is taking shape. Customers want to know how close they are to getting the product. Suppliers, partners want to know if they have to do anything or provide anything. There are so many demands on your time and you may not be able to update everyone personally. Thus the Product Owner needs to figure out the best way to introduce these updates to stakeholders, customers, teams etc. Is that via town halls, weekly emails or newsletters, posters or brown bag sessions? If you're not an expert who can decide what is best, hire a communications consultant. They can even write the content for you.

Establish the product vision, roadmap

We discussed the link between the strategy and the product in the previous chapters. The product strategy, vision, goals and roadmap are paramount. Without any clarity on these items, you are simply going to waste time and money. Hence organize the discovery sessions and clarify these items, as we discussed previously.

Kick off the product development

Declare it officially. Get everyone, stakeholders, potential customers, business owners, suppliers, vendors, the team, into a room or a conferencing space and kick off the product development. Organize a kickoff party. Share the product vision, roadmap, and the plan you are all going to follow. Bring the team to the stage, introduce them and the roles they will play. Put them in the spotlight. There is no better way to make them feel proud of being part of something bigger.

Ask the leaders to share their vision and strategy and why they think the product is important. When leaders show how keen they are about a product being developed, everyone will want to get involved to make it happen.

1	2 During the product development	3

Co-locate the product development team

At this stage, the product is in the development process. By now, all teams should be co-located. If not, you must arrange this. It may not be easy if you are in a corporate environment where traditional methods are generally used. If the process of co-locating the teams is difficult, you should get help from an Agile coach or Scrum Master.

Kick-off sprint zero

Sprint zero is the team's warm-up to get into the rhythm. You must all be operating on the cadence starting from day 1. You must have a proper sprint planning, set up the sprint priority and the goals and explain the prioritized user stories. The team should declare their velocity and pick the user stories according to priority and velocity.

Then the team will have daily stand-ups, updating the Kanban walls on progress and trying to achieve the sprint commitment. The Product Owner will do the backlog refinement in the middle of the sprint and help the team with the clarifications. At the end of the sprint, you must all do the sprint showcase and retrospective.

Your best friend in sprint zero is the Agile Coach. He/she will help you to get oriented with the agile practices and the cadence and he/she will help the team.

But be prepared. Prepared to be surprised. There will be chaos. There will be friction between team members. There will be disappointments and it will be an achievement if at least one user story is completed at the end of the sprint. Just know you are on the right track.

Sprint zero is meant to be like that. If you have a very good Agile coach, he/she will guide the team during the retrospective and come up with a plan for the next sprint. It will get better.

It may take some time for things to settle down and the team to deliver what has been committed. However, if you are following Agile correctly, with the right coaching, everything will be all right.

Refine the product backlog

This is one of the main responsibilities of the Product Owner during the development phase. The product backlog should be ready with enough details and new user stories to be selected in the next sprint. The Product Owner will probably need to write new user stories, new features and add acceptance criteria to the existing user stories. Priorities may have to be changed. Refining the product backlog is essential to make the next sprint a success.

Be available for the sprint planning, standups, retrospectives

These are team events where the Product Owner get updates from the team and the team receives updates from the Product Owner. Apart from these events, there should not be any other meetings which take up the team's working time. The Product Owner should make sure to be available for these events and utilize everyone's time efficiently.

During the development phase, the Product Owner will be extremely busy. There will be meetings with partners and suppliers, production issues to deal with and all sorts of other events. However, being available for the team should be one of the main priorities of the Product Owner. He/she must organize and plan other events and time in a way that gives the development team priority.

Conduct product showcases

Showcases are main events to give updates to the customers and stakeholder. If you are following the Agile methodology, the showcase should be the only meeting to update all the stakeholders. There is no point having status update meetings if there is no working product. It is just time-consuming to prepare and update reports. This is time the team and the Product Owner must spend developing the product to make it a working solution. Hence status updates should be organized as sprint showcases which showcase what the team has developed in the current sprint. When you maintain this event regularly at the end of every sprint, then all stakeholders will understand that it is a much better version of the status update meeting.

Communicate progress to sponsors, business owners and customers

There should be ways for sponsors, stakeholders, partners, suppliers and customers to get updates on the progress of the product. As we saw above, product showcase is the perfect event for that. But people may still have questions such as 'When will the new operating system be available?' or 'When will this particular issue be resolved?' or 'When can I expect this feature?' Hence the Product Owner should regularly communicate to the stakeholders on the progress of the product. This can be via emails or a collaborative space like Microsoft teams, a newsletter, or a Frequently Asked Questions (FAQ) type of portal. Encourage them to attend the showcase. For additional details, make these other channels available for them.

Adopt the lessons learnt, improvement suggestions

During the retrospectives and showcases, new improvement ideas will come up. If there are changes required to the backlog, or some experiments required and suggested by the team, they need be implemented. These might not be a direct product feature, but an improvement to the process. It is important to adapt the process where necessary. Hence the Product Owner should include these changes, updates and improvements along with the other product backlog features.

Measure the success of the product

Are you on the right track? Is the product reaching the goal? How many features have been implemented so far? How many more are there to implement? Are the customers happy? Is the business realizing its strategic goals? How do you know?

These are the questions the Product Owner should be able to answer by constantly monitoring and measuring. There is no point working for three months only to realize that none of the product features have yet been completed and released to the market. It should not take an entire year to discover that your customers are completely unhappy with the product. In the middle of development, you may lose track if you don't monitor and measure. The Product Owner should track the success and collect the data points to know how much progress you are all making.

This can be done in many ways. You can track the number of epics, features, user stories in each version of the product roadmap and see how many have been implemented as per the plan. If there is a deviation on the roadmap or the sprint plan, then it needs to be discussed and corrected. You need to collect customer feedback to measure the success of the product.

If there is no progress, then some decision-making is required. It may require some pivot, or it may even be the time to kill the product. But those decisions should be made sooner rather than later as you are burning company money. So, you should collect these metrics regularly and discuss the actions required with the right leaders.

Release on-demand

The product roadmap defines the plan of the product. It includes what features are developed and when they need to be released to the customers. This plan is an economical way to manage product release in a controlled environment. However, sometimes a product may need to be released outside these plans. For example, a sudden requirement from the client or an immediate bug fix. Hence at any time, whether planned or not, the product features should be able to be released 'on-demand'.

During product development, you should monitor such requirements and facilitate such release on-demand requests when necessary.

Decide if the product needs ramping down

Has the product achieved its target benefits or not? Is it adding value for the customers? What are they saying? Are they using the product for the intended purpose or have they shifted to a competitor product? Is your team spending a lot of time just to maintain the product?

The answers to these questions might hint to the Product Owner that it is time to retire the product. If the maintenance costs are higher than the returns (monitory or non-monetary) then it may be the right time. The Product Owner should monitor these metrics constantly so that product retirement actions can be determined well in advance. You may need to discuss the options with the leaders to decide the right actions.

Discuss the alternatives if the product needs to ramp down

If the decision has been made to ramp down the production,

there are still many things to do. Products cannot be stopped just like that because you thought that is the best option. There may be customers who are already using the product. They spent their money on the product because it was valuable to them. They may be using that product to run their business. As an example, let's say your product is a car engine. Suppliers are selling this car engine and they have stocks that they purchased from you. Customers are using the car engine you produce. What happens if you stop producing it and one of those customers reports an engine failure? It is not an easy process to stop product development. You have a responsibility to provide options for those customers. Hence the ramp down needs to be planned properly.

The Product Owner needs to decide who is going to be impacted, how much they are impacted and what options can be provided. These options should be investigated by collaborating with the business team.

Once the decision is made, options or alternatives should be developed and made available to the customers. This should all be communicated to the impacted parties well in advance.

Celebrate

Product development is a stressful job. Not only for you, but also for your team, it can be very tough. There is a lot of pressure to meet commitments, but milestones can help the team to realize that those tough times are for a good cause. Hence make it a habit to celebrate success often.

Bring your customers, suppliers, partners and team together to be one team. Customers would like to know the team and the team would love to see how their efforts have benefited customers. Give awards to those who deserve them. Acknowledge success as well as failures. Let the customers and suppliers know the path you have followed. Find different ways to celebrate at regular intervals. It is vital and it creates a different vibe and a way to bond with your team and the other partners.

1	2	3 During product disposal

At this stage, the Product Owner has either stopped production or is planning to stop it in a few weeks' or months' time. Still, your job as the Product Owner is not done. Even after finishing the product development, there are multiple activities you must complete as explained below.

Integrate lessons learnt into sharing across the organization

What you have just gone through is a unique experience. This may be the first product you have developed using Agile as a methodology. Even if is not the first product, every product is unique in an organizational setup. Your entire team may have spent more than six months working on this product, which is a significant investment for the organization. There must be many lessons learnt during the journey.

Did the Product Owner start the product in the right way? Was Agile as a method successful? Did the team have the right skills? Was this the right strategy? What tools were valuable and what were not? If the Product Owner were to begin again, what would he/she do differently? Did you have the right suppliers/partners? Would you change them if you were to start over?

The responses to these questions will be very valuable for the rest of the organization, teams, and partners/suppliers. The Product Owner should share these lessons with the organization and, if applicable, with the customers. It will help the organization when they develop the next set of strategies and the new line of products.

Ensure stakeholder/customer queries are answered and some sort of mechanism is available for them to be connected

Even if the product is out of production and service, customers and stakeholders may be thinking that it is still in production. They may have queries and may try to connect with the Product Owner or the production teams. Hence at least update them that the product no longer exists. Remember customers try to reach the Product Owner because they have some relationship with the product, and they should be valued. Connect with them and when they have queries, answer or direct them to someone who can provide accurate information.

Ensure performance reviews/rewards are given to the team

Your team has been working with this product for a long time. It may even be a few years. When you decide to stop the product, it impacts your team. They might have been so involved with the product work that this decision will be very disappointing. So, make sure you update them well in advance.

They may need to be moved into other teams or some of them, like contractors, might even have to find new jobs. So, you need to manage it very responsibly.

At the same time, you should make sure that they have received the right performance feedback. If they have been hired internally their managers can be updated with this feedback. They will be measured based on the work they have done, and some will even have a bonus because of their performance. Thus, the Product Owner should give the credits/reviews/feedback appropriately. Let them know how much you value them and what incredible things they have done with the product.

CHAPTER 11
ANTI-AGILE PATTERNS
RELEVANT TO PRODUCT OWNER

In this section, we will try to build insight on commonly visible anti-Agile patterns originating from product management and Product Owner(PO)s. As Agile is a relatively new way of working and difficult to implement, we may fall back on the old way of working in the process of moving to Agile. When I say the old way of working, I mean the traditional way which uses phase by phase development and takes a long time to deliver products.

Having a good knowledge of anti-Agile patterns will help the Product Owner to realize if they are going back to the non-productive way of working.

When you take up the role of Product Owner and make yourself accountable for strategic implementation, pay attention to these patterns because they can negatively impact product development, delivery, and your career too. Throughout the process, don't hesitate to get help from the enterprise or senior Agile coach if you recognize these anti-Agile patterns.

Not having a Product Owner

The number of products which start without a Product Owner is countless. We see this in large organizations. Leaders say, 'just start and we'll find a Product Owner'.

Think of all the Product Owner's responsibilities I mentioned previously. What happens if there is no Product Owner? Who decides the strategy, product vision and goals? Who are the stakeholders? What is the product roadmap? These are not questions team members can answer on their own.

Product development, as you have read in the previous chapters, is highly strategic, operational work. The Scrum Master or the team members cannot do that work because it requires a different skillset.

If a Product Owner cannot be selected internally or externally for various reasons (unavailability, budget, skillset) then the product may not be at the right level of prioritization. If you are part of such a team, request that leaders stop the initiative until the Product Owner is found. This is the best thing to do.

Having multiple Product Owners in the same squad/ Agile team

Having multiple Product Owners for one product backlog brings the same consequences as not having a Product Owner for a product. (Just to be clear, this anti–Agile pattern only refers to having multiple Product Owners in one squad or one team or a product backlog). Surprisingly, I have seen many product setups where two or sometimes three Product Owners are assigned to the same squad or backlog. This happens when the Agile maturity of the organization is still low.

According to Scrum.org:

> 'The Product Owner is one person, not a committee. The Product Owner may represent the desires of a committee in the Product Backlog, but those wanting to change a Product Backlog item's priority must address the Product Owner' (Scrum.Org, 2020).

When there are multiple Product Owners per product and the backlog, most of the time there are conflicts of interest and clashes of authority. For example, if a Product Owner is assigned from the IT side and another from the business side, there will be conflicts when they must choose user stories. Which one should have a higher priority? A new business product feature or a technical refactoring user story? The IT Product Owner will normally have a bias towards the refactoring while the business Product Owner wants to see the business product feature implemented. Egos will clash. We have seen this happen in the workplace and it makes teams go nowhere.

Therefore it is necessary to appoint only one Product Owner per squad or per product. It is possible to have multiple subject matter experts assigned to the product, but when it comes to Product Ownership there should be only one Product Owner. If Agile is mature within the organization, everyone understands the responsibilities of a Product Owner and they know Product Ownership is not a shared responsibility. In these organizations, management will make sure that only one person is assigned to a squad as a Product Owner.

When the product is larger in scale and has multiple features developed by different teams it needs to be structured something like below. There is a Product Owner per squad, and they manage the team backlog or feature backlog. All are synchronized to the product backlog and Chief Product Owner.

The Chief Product Owner owns the entire product, but each of the features is owned by Product Owners 1, 2, 3, and 4 respectively.

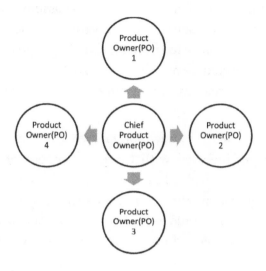

Figure 50 : Product ownership of a bigger product

Product Owners working in isolation

As we discussed in previous chapters, developing a product involves many parties; the customers, suppliers, and internal stakeholders like sales, marketing, supply chain, logistics, IT, finance, and legal personnel. Depending on the type of product, some or all the above parties may be involved.

Systems thinking, which is the end-to-end cycle of the product, is critical in building a good product. For example, once the product has been developed, it needs to be sent to the right market, to the right segment and the right customer. This may be done via the marketing department. While the product is being marketed, it needs to have a pricing structure, and that calls for the involvement of the pricing team in marketing and finance, who will consider financial components such as product costs, profit margins, and so on. In short, everyone associated with the workstream has a role to play.

A product developed without involving everyone may miss

many important points. It means that many assumptions will have been made about the touchpoints of various value stream items, and with so many omissions there is a huge possibility of the product being rejected hence delay to market. Thus, the Product Owner must be proactive in getting everyone involved in the processes.

There are many touchpoints where the rest of the functions can get involved with the development of the product. Stakeholders can be involved in discovery sessions at the beginning of the project and a showcase at the end of respective iterations. The Product Owner should define a way to keep them involved, engaged, and updated throughout the product development process.

If leaders, Scrum Masters, or team leaders feel that the product is being developed in isolation, they should initiate team discussions, discuss the negative impact and get the Product Owner to work with other teams.

No product vision or roadmap

If there is no product vision and roadmap, there is no clear direction for the product. If the direction cannot be articulated, it may still be at the conceptual level. It may even be at the ideation stage.

One of the biggest mistakes organizations make is jumping into the solution without even understanding the real problem. They spend millions of dollars only to realize that they are not addressing the actual problem. Creating a product vision, product model and roadmap helps to consolidate the stakeholders' knowledge and expectations to define what they are going to do.

Hence if the Scrum Master, leaders or the team see that there is no product vision or roadmap, they should work as a team to create one.

Focusing only on short-term goals

The roadmap is generally the 'how to get there' plan. The entire product development duration is broken down into small, incremental deliveries, usually as quarterly releases. Some fast-paced products may be more aggressive in terms of releases, where the plan is to release some product features every month.

Most Product Owners try to deliver something in each sprint. They tend to focus on 'low hanging fruits'. Research conducted by Karlstrom and Runeson, 2005 et al., by analyzing product development in Ericson, ABB and Vodafone had a similar finding. Such short-term focus may not deliver the results planned at the strategic level. There is no point in delivering something if it is not part of the end goal. You must always keep the end goal in mind when planning the sprint deliverables.

One way to avoid such anti-Agile patterns is always to create the roadmap based on the customer journey map and user story mapping. The product backlog can be prioritized based on the user story mapping and user stories selected for the next sprint.

Always analyze the benefits realized at feature and epic level. When the epics and features were created, the Product Owner should have outlined the benefits each epic and feature need to deliver when implemented. At the end of each sprint, and a release, the Product Owner should measure the returns gained as per the plan. If there are no returns or incremental returns based on the measurement identified by the Product Owner (for example, revenue, number of product downloads, customer satisfaction index etc.), then the product is not developing as planned. Some analysis is required to identify why.

Skipping backlog refinement/grooming

In the previous chapters, we discussed the importance of an up-to-date product backlog. If the product backlog is not updated with the priorities and the necessary details for the next immediate sprint, then the team may produce low priority work. What I have seen is that many Product Owners remember the product backlog prioritization just a few minutes before the sprint planning session. Then they just shuffle the items in a hurry without any proper rationalization.

Most Product Owner(PO)s start well and do backlog refinement at the beginning of the project. However, as the project advances, he/she becomes extremely busy with the team as well as the external stakeholders, and the tendency is to forget about it. This produces waste and demotivates the team because of their wasted effort. The Product Owner may not be able to answer questions asked by the team or clarify any acceptance criteria.

The following are some ways to avoid falling into this anti-Agile pattern.

- The Product Owner can set a designated time in his/her calendar for product refinement. Every week, he/she can schedule a good two hours, probably in the middle of the week. A calendar invitation will remind the Product Owner to sit and go through the strategy, vision, roadmap and the new trends coming up which should be reflected in the backlog. When the Product Owner is forced to take time in this way, this event will start to become a habit.

- The Product Owner can get help from the team to do the refinement. He/she can collaborate with the team but cannot delegate this. Get the Scrum Master, senior technical leader and other stakeholders into this weekly meeting to have their input as well.

- The Product Owner can get help from the business analyst in digging up details and making the required documentation. However, decision-making should not be delegated.

Not writing acceptance criteria

Acceptance criteria are very critical information relevant to the quality of the product features. If the Product Owner does not write acceptance criteria for product features and user stories, he/she may be causing rework and delays.

These acceptance criteria play a major role in the development and testing of the features. For example, if an acceptance criterion says, 'search should return the query results within two seconds', it gives an indication of the code and query optimization the developer must use.

Acceptance criteria often stem from stakeholders' and customers' expectations for the product. To meet these expectations, they need to be contacted before the sprint planning takes place. Writing acceptance criteria for every user story is required so that the team knows in advance how the story should be developed.

Product Owner not attending sprint planning

We have seen an increase in the number of sprint planning sessions where the Product Owner does not attend at all. This is a nearly four-hour session, so Product Owners who have not understood the criticality of sprint planning will try to skip it, saying that the product backlog is up to date and prioritized. Sometimes responsibility is delegated to someone else, such as the business analyst. This is an anti-Agile pattern which produces waste. Let's see why.

The entire product development duration is short compared to traditional product development such as Waterfall. In Agile development, a lot happens within just two weeks.

During a sprint a product feature can be completed. During the sprint planning session, the team shares various information and decision-making conversations take place between the team, the Product Owner and the Scrum Master. The Product Owner who owns the features has a whole lot of information about business background, customer requirements and acceptance criteria, so if he/she is not available for sprint planning, the team will not receive this information.

Hence make sure the sprint planning is not skipped. Block the session well in advance. It can be set up as a recurring event in the calendar.

Product Owner assigning tasks to the team

Agile is an environment that promotes self-organization. A cross-functional team works with the Product Owner to deliver the priorities set by him/her. The point to note here is that this is a collaboration. The team decides how to implement the priorities based on the user stories prioritized by the Product Owner.

A mature Agile team knows how to breakdown user stories into tasks and distribute them among the team equally. This is shocking to some managers who think the team cannot work without their instructions. Some Product Owners and even Scrum Masters who transition from traditional control driven environments try to tell the team what to do and how to do it, a sort of micromanagement.

Such habits do not allow the team to be self-organized and as a result, they will always be waiting until someone asks them to do something. Instead, they should be allowed to take control of the things they have to do. The Product Owner's job is only to tell them which product features have the highest priority, why they have priority and the acceptance criteria.

It's the team's job to break down the user stories, estimate their size, pick user stories to meet their velocity and organize the tasks amongst themselves. They can do that only if the Product Owner allows them to. You should pay close attention to see if you are following this anti-Agile pattern, and if so, make a conscious effort not to be a control-freak.

Being a Product Owner for multiple products

In most corporate environments, we find the Product Owner being assigned to multiple products. In such situations, the Product Owner is a shared resource. Although we understand resource and budget limitations, assigning a Product Owner for multiple products or features is a recipe for the products to fail. In the end, a lot of money is spent creating waste instead of delivering benefits to the customer. As we have seen in the previous chapters, the Product Owner is quite hands-on with one team and is a busy person. He/she may even struggle to have enough time for one team. If that is the case, how is he/she going to support another product feature?

How to avoid the anti-pattern?

Don't try to be a superhero. If you, as the Product Owner, are asked to take over two or three teams or multiple products, as an Agile practitioner you should be able to lead by Agile values and practices. Be the change agent for the rest of the organization. Explain to the leaders why it is not a viable option and how it would compromise the product success. The Product Owner should have the courage to say No when required.

Skipping sprint reviews or showcases

The product showcase is the event where the team showcases the product feature they have built in the previous sprint. During this event the team members explain the sprint goal, the features they implemented, and the issues they encountered during development. If they could not implement some promised features, they explain why.

The event provides stakeholders with the chance to interact with the product. The session is interactive. Attendees, in turn, have the chance to ask questions, validate their assumptions, and understand what it is that slows down the app.

For the Product Owner, this event is not optional. It is your product; hence you need to be there. The Product Owner must see the implemented features, and if any features were not implemented as per the commitment, he/she needs to know the reason. Also, the Product Owner has the responsibility to respond to some stakeholder questions. Overall, it is a major issue if the Product Owner fails to attend a showcase.

Combining the Product Owner and Scrum Master jobs

We have seen situations where the Product Owner and Scrum Master roles are combined, especially if resources are scarce. This is not a good arrangement and should not be encouraged at all. Ideally, all roles need to be properly defined, and the right individuals assigned to each. The skillset required for each role is unique, and roles should be matched with the right individuals.

Scrum Master is a unique and critical role for the success of the product. The Scrum Master has an equal, or an even greater workload, in terms of effort needed to steer the Agile process in the right direction and coach the Product Owner and the team on Agile. Scrum Masters may have the skillset to take on the PO role, but in terms of effort, time and focus, both roles cannot be combined successfully. Our research demonstrates that products don't deliver on time and provide the necessary customer 'wow factors' when both roles are combined. Hence this anti-Agile pattern should be avoided at any cost.

Pivoting the sprint

Every sprint has a goal. Within the short period of one, two, three or four weeks, the team has to achieve the sprint goal that the Product Owner has established. Once they agree, the team goes into the mission of achieving this. However, sometimes we have seen the sprint goal being abandoned in the middle of the sprint, and the team has to start from scratch. When that happens, everything that has been achieved up until then may be discarded.

Unfortunately, this happens quite frequently, and it is, therefore, an issue that must be addressed. For example, if there is pivoting in every sprint, there is the possibility that the team is not achieving anything constructive towards the final product as planned. Sometimes pivoting may be wise. But it needs to happen early and should have a rationale and be avoided where possible. If it happens too frequently, the Product Owner or Scrum Master needs to be vigilant, to understand the root cause.

How to avoid this anti-Agile pattern:

- Analyze dependencies, risks and assumptions

  When developing the product roadmap, identify the list of assumptions made, associated risks and dependencies. Then validate them. Involve the relevant parties so they can do the validation early in the project, helping to unlock the dependencies and validate assumptions. That way, ambiguities and unknown factors can be minimized.

- Have shorter sprints

  If the product is dependent on different research, and the research often affects the direction of the sprint, then it would be wise to make the sprints shorter. Sprints of one week are ideal in such situations.

- Consider doing spikes instead of taking up full-blown work

  One way to validate assumptions or unknowns is by doing a spike. A spike is just a small set of tasks to validate the assumptions or technical feasibility. It does not entail producing a shippable product. It helps to validate whether the concept or the assumptions are doable or not. The spike could involve just a few lines of code instead of the full solution.

Whatever the cause of the deviation, it is necessary to take control of the situation to avoid waste.

Delegating Product Owner responsibilities to business analysts

There is a lot of confusion and misunderstandings surrounding the role of business analyst. Some delegate Product Owner responsibilities to business analysts. They are not Product Owners. Business analysts can do business process analysis, understand how a certain business function works, create process flows and articulate that in generic layman language. Often business analysts are the proxies for business. In most IT products, business analysts work between two layers. However, this does not mean business analysts have the necessary knowledge or authority to make decisions on product vision, strategy, and the product roadmap.

Business analysts, however, can help the Product Owner with the necessary analysis and market and customer research required, so that he/she can obtain the right amount of details. But always keep in mind that these are two very distinct roles.

Summary

As we discussed throughout this book, Agile is a new way of working. It demands a lot of new behaviors. This applies to Product Owners as well. When Product Owners are new to the Agile way of working, they can easily slip back into the old style of working. This is the main reason Agile will not achieve expected results. Hence, when you are a Product Owner you should check regularly whether you are guilty of any of the anti-Agile patterns listed above. In addition, discuss with a Scrum Master and try to understand what practices you need to cultivate. It is essential that Product Owners get this coaching from Scrum Masters. Scrum Masters are the Agile process owners so they should be able to guide the Product Owners when anti-Agile patterns occur

References:

Karlstrom and Runeson, 2005 - Karlstrom and Runeson, 2006, Karlstrom and Runeson, 2005, Karlstrom and Runeson, 2006 Combining Agile methods with Stage-Gate project management,

D. Karlstrom and P. RunesonIEEE software (2005), pp. 43-49 (May–June)

BEYOND THE BOOK

This book aims to help Product Owners get a good grip on Agile. After reading the book, you may need some further clarification or have feedback. I encourage you to subscribe to our website and submit your comments and queries.

ABOUT THE AUTHOR

Anusha Hewage is the founder of AgilityDNA, a consulting business dedicated to providing enterprise Agile services. Anusha is also the founder of AgileBusinessSchool, an executive business school providing Agile and project management training.

She is an authentic business leader with over two decades of industry experience in various Fortune 100 companies, in both global and regional capacities.

Anusha has specialized in major program/project management, portfolio management, risk management, digital business transformation, organizational management, and change management.

Anusha is a strong believer in people and purpose-driven initiatives and so she focuses on developing effective leaders.

Anusha has over a decade of experience in Agile, conducting various Agile transformation programs across several organizations. She is a Certified Scaled Program Consultant (SAFe-SPC), Certified Scrum Master, Agile Certified Practitioner (PMI-ACP), Enterprise Agile coach , trainer and a researcher.

Anusha holds a Master's degree from the University of Oxford, United Kingdom, and Charles Stuart University, Australia.

Contact her at: agilitydna@gmail.com

Subscribe and follow her on social media via:

https://agilitydna.com

OTHER BOOKS BY THE AUTHOR

Becoming a Scrum Master – Everything you should know to be a GREAT Scrum Master

Anti-Agile Patterns: Get your Agile Transformation back on track

First Time Manager: New Manager's Guidebook